PENGUIN BOOKS

A GRAND ILLUSION?

Tony Judt is the Erich Maria Remarque Professor of European Studies at New York University. He is a frequent contributor to the *New York Review of Books*.

KU-114-537

# TONY JUDT

# A GRAND ILLUSION

## AN ESSAY ON EUROPE

PENGUIN BOOKS

PENGUIN BOOKS

Published by the Penguin Group
Penguin Books Ltd, 27 Wrights Lane, London W8 5TZ, England
Penguin Books USA Inc., 375 Hudson Street, New York, New York 10014, USA
Penguin Books Australia Ltd, Ringwood, Victoria, Australia
Penguin Books Canada Ltd, 10 Alcorn Avenue, Toronto, Ontario, Canada M4V 3B2
Penguin Books (NZ) Ltd, 182–190 Wairau Road, Auckland 10, New Zealand

Penguin Books Ltd, Registered Offices: Harmondsworth, Middlesex, England

First published simultaneously in the USA by Hill and Wang and in Canada by
HarperCollinsCanada Ltd 1996
Published in Penguin Books 1997
1 3 5 7 9 10 8 6 4 2

Printed in England by Clays Ltd, St Ives plc

# CONTENTS

# PREFACE

THIS BOOK is based on lectures I gave at the Johns Hopkins Center in Bologna in May 1995, under the auspices of *The New York Review of Books* and Hill and Wang. I should like to thank the director of the Center, Professor Robert Evans, for his hospitality, and Professor Pietro Corsi, editor of *La Rivista dei Libri*, for helping to organize and sponsor the series. The lively discussions that followed the lectures were most helpful, and I hope that in what follows it will be clear how much I have learned from them. The original idea for the book came out of conversations with Robert Silvers and Elisabeth Sifton, and I am especially grateful to them both for their suggestions and their encouragement.

More than an occasional piece, but much less than a history, this book is really an attempt to address three contemporary questions: What are the prospects for the European Union? If they are not wholly rosy, why is that? And how much does it, in any event, matter whether a united Europe may or may not come about? The cast of the questions, and the answers I shall propose, may seem to mark me as a Euro-skeptic, the more so because I am British—by nationality if not by residence. Against that charge I should like to plead a preemptive innocence. I am enthusiastically European; no informed person could seriously wish to return to the embattled, mutually antagonistic circle of suspicious and introverted nations that was the European continent in the quite recent past. Whatever moves us away from *that* Europe is good, and the further the better.

But it is one thing to think an outcome desirable, quite another to suppose it possible. And it is my contention in this essay that a truly united Europe is sufficiently unlikely for it to be unwise and self-defeating to insist upon it. I am thus, I suppose, a Euro-pessimist. Unlike Jean Monnet, the founder of the European Community, I don't believe that it is prudent, or possible, to "exorcise history," at any rate beyond moderate limits, and my essay thus concludes with a plea for the partial reinstatement, or relegitimation, of nation-states. For the same reasons I have tried to argue that whether or not the future of formerly Communist states in Eastern Europe *ought* to lie within a fully integrated Europe, the fact is that this may not come to pass; it might therefore be the better part of wisdom to stop promising otherwise.

The argument of this book, and its tone, are much influenced by the fact that it was written in Austria. The prospects for Europe, and its coming difficulties, look a little different in the center of the continent than they do on the western fringe, where most of the institutions of European union are to be found. The imperial inheritance and contemporary provinciality of central Europe, the overwhelming presence of Germany, the proximity of "former Yugoslavia," and the ease with which one may cross the ancient east–west divide and see just how very different the two Europes still are, all contribute to a more clouded prospect for union than the one that beckons farther north or west. I am thus especially grateful to New York University for granting me sabbatical leave and to the Institut für die Wissenschaften vom Menschen and its director, Professor Krzystof Michalski, for generously inviting me to spend it as their guest in Vienna.

*Vienna, January 1996*

# A GRAND ILLUSION?

# 1

# A GRAND ILLUSION

THE EUROPEAN Coal and Steel Community was born in 1951 from an idea conceived by Jean Monnet and proposed by Robert Schuman, the French Foreign Minister, in May 1950. In 1958 it became the European Economic Community, popularly referred to as the "Europe of Six" (France, West Germany, Italy, and the Benelux countries). This prosperous, "far-western" Europe then took in the United Kingdom, Denmark, and Ireland to become the "Europe of Nine," after which it grew larger still and became the "Europe of Twelve" with the addition in the 1980s of Greece, Spain, and Portugal. The most recent members—Austria, Sweden, and Finland—bring its number to fifteen. When people refer to possible future adherents they now quite simply and unblushingly speak of a country—Slovenia, Poland—"joining Europe."

This curious locution shows how much Europe today is not so much a place as an idea, a peaceful, prosperous, international community of shared interests and collaborating parts; a "Europe of the mind," of human rights, of the free movement of goods, ideas, and persons, of ever-greater cooperation and unity. The emergence of this hyper-real Europe, more European than the continent itself, an inward and future projection of all the higher values of the ancient civilization but shorn of its darker qualities, cannot be attributed just to the imprisonment of Europe's other, eastern, half under Communism. After all, not only the people's democracies stood apart from this new "Europe" but also Switzerland, Norway, and (until recently) Austria and Sweden, exemplars of many of the social and civic virtues that "Europeans" have been seeking to embody in their new institutions. If we are to understand the sources—and, as I shall argue, the limitations and perhaps the risks—of this "Europe" now held before us as guide and promise, we must go back to a moment in the recent past when the prospects for any kind of Europe looked particularly grim.

It is an understandable mistake to suppose, in retrospect, that postwar Western Europe was rebuilt by idealists for a united continent. Such people unquestionably existed, belonging to organizations like the European Unity Movement of 1947. But they had no discernible real-world impact. In a curious way it was British leaders, who were to play no active role in the actual construction of European unity in the years to come, who had the most to say on the subject of a unified continent: in October 1942 Prime Minister Winston Churchill noted to Anthony Eden, the British Foreign Secretary, that "it would be a measureless disaster if Russian bolshevism overlaid the culture and independence of the ancient states of Europe. Hard as it is to say now, I trust that the European family may act unitedly as one, under a Council of Europe."[1] There certainly *was* an idealist mood in 1945 across the liberated lands of continental Europe, but the goals of most of its spokesmen were domestic: change and reform at home, along lines set down by the various coalitions that had come together during the war to form resistance movements against Nazi occupation. Well into the 1950s it was uncommon to find intellectuals or politicians in Europe interested primarily in the future of a united continent rather than in the politics of their own country.

If it was not idealism that drove Europeans in those years, nor was it the manifest imperatives of historical destiny. Very little in the postwar years suggested a natural or inevitable coming together of the survivors of Hitler's war. In 1944 the American journalist Janet Flanner, in one of her regular dispatches for *The New Yorker*, foresaw rather the opposite: a coming era of intra-European competition for scarce resources among desperate nations. That the states of Western Europe would need to cooperate in some way was of course obvious; but the extent and the forms of that cooperation

---

1. Churchill would go on to make speeches about a united Europe after the war as well, in Zurich in September 1946 and at London's Albert Hall in May 1947. But like most British politicians he imagined and wanted little more than a meeting place and talking shop, which is what the "Council of Europe" eventually became and has remained.

were not inscribed in the mere fact of postwar exhaustion and collective destitution. And many possible forms of cooperation, economic ones in particular, had nothing idealistic about them and carried no implications of future unity.

Indeed, the idea of pooling economic interests to overcome common problems was far from new. A "United States" of Europe had even been proposed by some in the mid-nineteenth century (it was advocated by *Le Moniteur*, a newspaper of the French Second Republic, in February 1848). There were various proposals to model an economic federation of Europe along Swiss cantonal lines. Zollvereins—customs unions—were another popular theme in nineteenth-century discussions; there were proposals to extend the German customs union, established in 1834, to include the Netherlands, Belgium, Denmark, and even the Habsburg lands, though these proposals got nowhere.

The subject of trade agreements attracted renewed attention after World War I, when the breakup of empires and the resulting disruption of production units and trade patterns made the need for cartels and trading pacts seem urgent, as did the depreciation of currencies and depression of prices that marked the early 1920s (there was also more than a hint of anti-Americanism, a fear of U.S. competition; this would continue to favor and to haunt intra-European trade agreements to the present day). The best known of the resulting agreements was the International Steel Cartel signed in September 1926 and covering Germany, France, Belgium, Luxembourg, and the Saarland (then still separated from Germany under the terms of the Versailles Treaty). It was joined by Czechoslovakia, Austria, and Hungary a year later. Renounced by German producers in 1929, it was abandoned two years later at the height of the Depression.

Other, similar efforts were made to shore up the interwar European economy—the so-called Oslo Group of 1930 (covering Scandinavian and Benelux countries) and the Rome Protocol of 1934 signed by Italy, Hungary, and Austria. None of these prevented the collapse of trade, the main source and indicator of economic stagnation; from 1929 to 1936 French trade to Germany fell by 80 percent, German exports to France by 85 percent. But it is significant that as late as 1938 French and Germans were still forlornly trying to shore things up with a (never-to-be-ratified) trading agreement under which France would take more German chemical and engineering output in return for increased German importation of French agricultural produce.

Accompanying these unsteady and unsuccessful attempts at economic partnership were diplomatic efforts, notably by the French statesman Aristide Briand and his German counterpart Gustav Stresemann, to bring about greater Franco-German cooperation. During the 1920s Stresemann argued tirelessly for an end to customs barriers and even the creation of a Eurocurrency. If he didn't quite share the convictions of Walther Rathenau, the

German cabinet minister murdered by nationalists in 1922, who according to Stefan Zweig "staked his life" on the idea of Europe, Stresemann undoubtedly appreciated that the Germans' own interests were best served by setting them in a broader, European context. Briand was characteristically more expansive if imprecise; his 1929 plan for a United Europe argued that "among peoples constituting geographical groups, like the peoples of Europe, there should be some kind of federal bond." A British Foreign Office commentary on the Briand proposal was perceptive if skeptical: it represented a "regrouping and consolidation of European finance and industry [such] as to assure France and the rest of Europe against the ever-growing strength of non-European and especially American competition. This is primarily what has always been meant by the 'United States of Europe' or 'pan Europe' and without this it is hard to see that the word 'pan-Europe' can mean anything at all."[2]

There was thus no shortage of precedents for postwar Europe's eventual quest for economic unity, and nothing especially idealist about the revival of these ideas and projects in due course. On the contrary, interest in a revival of the depressed continent by transnational organization was widespread across the political spectrum. Throughout the interwar years Fascists especially, but

2. Quoted in the editor's introduction to P. Stirk, ed., *European Unity in Context: The Inter-war Period* (London, 1989), p. 13.

not only Fascists, had spoken and written of the goal of a renewed, rejuvenated Europe, shorn of its ancient divisions and united around a common set of goals and institutions. Young neutralists in the 1930s—such as the Belgian Socialist Paul-Henri Spaak, a future Belgian foreign minister and European statesman—joined organizations of the thirties with names like Jeune Europe, where they met others of similar mind, including Otto Abetz, the future German ambassador in occupied Paris.

In the 1920s the driving motive behind the idea of European unity was pacifism; the authors of a 1922 manifesto in favor of a United Europe argued that in a unified Europe there would be no more wars. It is not altogether a coincidence that a prominent signatory of this manifesto should have been the young Frenchman Jean Luchaire, later to edit the leading collaborationist newspaper in Vichy France. By the end of the Second World War discussion of a united Europe carried grimmer connotations: Albert Speer's plans for a New European Order, a new Continental System based on Germany, had been echoed in a thousand wartime speeches, where visions of a new Europe did sinister service as a synonym for anti-Bolshevism, collaboration with National Socialism, and rejection of the old liberal, democratic, and divided prewar world.

Not surprisingly, then, there was little talk of a "united Europe" in the first years after the defeat of Germany: the terminology was polluted. The makers of postwar Europe were driven instead by realistic, national

motives of the most conventional and traditional kind
—which is hardly surprising when one considers that
most of them had grown up in a world of nation-states
and alliances, their earliest adult memories dating back
before the First World War. They could only imagine
the alternatives facing them after 1945 in the light of
earlier experiences and mistakes and plan accordingly.

For the French, the dilemma facing them after 1945
was not fundamentally different from that of 1918, except that in the latter case France had at least been
among the victors, whereas in 1945 it was in all but
name a defeated country. Fearing abandonment by their
Anglo-American allies, de Gaulle and other French politicians in 1945, like Clemenceau in 1919, had once
again to resolve their German dilemma: how to hold
German power down to an unthreatening level while
keeping Germany productive enough to ensure a suffi-
cient flow of vital raw materials to keep French industry
alive. For France was uniquely dependent on German
resources—coal in particular—and had been since the
1890s. In order to fire its own steel, France needed coal
from the Ruhr; ironically, the return of Alsace-Lorraine
after 1919 had increased this dependence, since the
recaptured territories doubled French steel-making capacity without adding significantly to the country's coal
supplies. By 1938 France was the world's biggest im-
porter of coal and imported 420,000 tons per month
from the Ruhr alone. By 1946, however, the supply of
Ruhr coal was down by 70 percent, at a time when

France's own coal production was well below its 1929 level.

French strategy, then, required the urgent exploitation of German resources, and the initial French postwar plan was simply to reduce Germany's political and military means to the minimum while exploiting its raw materials to the full—a replay of the unsuccessful strategy that had led to France's occupation of the Ruhr in 1923. This forlorn wish to replicate the disastrous policies of the early 1920s was incompatible with the desire of British and American political leaders to revive the (west) German economy—partly for the sake of European recovery, but also to relieve the British in particular of the cost of feeding and housing the people in their zone of occupation. Moreover, the British and the Americans (notably the U.S. military commander in Berlin, General Lucius Clay) were increasingly disposed to accord to the western zone of postwar Germany a degree of autonomy, a policy with which the French were understandably uncomfortable (the British and Americans were willing for the French to control the Saarland, but the coal there was largely unsuitable for French domestic needs).

French leaders such as Georges Bidault tried to work around this impediment by allying with the U.S.S.R. in a series of meetings during 1946 and 1947, an echo of the traditional French diplomatic strategy of associating with a strong power to the east of Germany. There was some logic in this—the Soviets were in favor of exploiting to the full the assets of their own zone of occupied Germany and had no objection to the French benefiting from West German resources, especially if this antagonized the Americans and the British. But with the onset of the Cold War the Russians had less use for the (in any case limited) services afforded them by French diplomatic maneuvering, and at a Moscow meeting in April 1947 Foreign Minister Vyacheslav Molotov brusquely rejected France's plans for dismantling Germany, leaving Paris with no recourse but to adopt a third strategy.

This consisted of accepting the need for a revived West German economy and a unified West German state, but hedging it around with international alliances, economic agreements, and other penumbra, while ensuring French access to its potential wealth, vital for the success of the newly conceived Monnet Plan—a program for French industrial reconstruction that depended crucially upon available and affordable German raw materials. Hence the complicated negotiations of 1949 and 1950 between France and its various would-be partners: Italy, the Benelux countries, and Great Britain. In their original form these discussions might have come close to reproducing the French-dominated, trade-restricting tariff agreements of the interwar years, with the added benefit of securing French access to German raw materials on terms never before possible. The role of the British in such an entity would of course have been primarily to guarantee France (and its other continental partners) against the future threat of a revived and overpowerful Germany.

But these proposals got nowhere, and the French were left with neither an agreement covering West Germany *and* Britain, nor one that excluded Germany. The result was the Schuman Plan, based on Jean Monnet's scheme for a six-nation community that would share and regulate production and consumption of coal and steel under an autonomous international authority. Announced by Robert Schuman, France's Foreign Minister, this proposal took the imaginative leap of accepting the absence of Great Britain from its proposed European Coal and Steel Community while retaining the participation of West Germany. Such a resolution of the French dilemma would have been unthinkable just a few years earlier, and even in 1950 it was distinctly a second-best solution, the British absence being a source of much regret to the Dutch negotiators in particular (though the Schuman Plan did have the merit of giving France a chance to take the initiative without informing London—sweet revenge after a decade of diplomatic humiliation, from Munich to Moscow).

Indeed, the French in 1950, like the nineteenth-century Habsburgs who opted for a dominant role in central and southeastern Europe only after they had been edged out of German affairs by Prussia, accepted the "European" solution to their German problem only after their preferred strategies had been thwarted by the other powers. The idea was not wholly new—Edouard Herriot, the leader of the ill-starred Cartel des Gauches, (1924–26), had indicated a similar willingness to commit France to a "united Europe" once the "German problem" was addressed. But in 1925 France had been in no position to impose a "European" solution to its difficulties—and anyway had felt no urgent need to do so. Even in the aftermath of France's third war with Germany in seventy-five years, its allies showed little sympathy for France's continuing worries about an overmighty Germany: according to U.S. Secretary of State George C. Marshall, in 1948, "French preoccupation with Germany as a major threat . . . seems to us outmoded and unrealistic."

Nonetheless, and in spite of themselves, the French were successful beyond their wildest hopes in "Europeanizing" their historical difficulty by incorporating West Germany into a Francocentric community where France got what its leaders thought it needed without appearing to have done so by conventionally selfish means. As Jacques Delors, the French politician who was to end his public career as President of the European Commission, put it many years later, in a revealing passage from his aptly titled book *La France par l'Europe* (1988), "Creating Europe is a way of regaining that margin of liberty necessary for a 'certain idea of France.'" But this was possible not only because Germany was in no position to object but also because, for special and contingent reasons, the authorities in Bonn wanted the same thing.

As the West German Chancellor Konrad Adenauer put it when he was first told of the Schuman Plan, "This is our breakthrough." Only through such a "supernational" entity could the new Federal Republic of Germany hope to reenter the international community on equal terms. From the beginning, West Germany (like France's other partners) would have preferred a broader union, one that included Britain, but acceded to the European Coal and Steel Community on French terms as a first step in obtaining French support for its own objectives—notably, increased sovereignty.[3]

The motives of France's partners are equally revealing. Like France, but perhaps more so, the Netherlands and Belgium were initially worried that after the war the United States might retreat from Europe: in the years 1945–47 there were real fears of a repeat of American isolationism as the vast majority of U.S. troops were withdrawn and the U.S. electorate showed a consistently high level of uninterest in European affairs. Hence the Benelux countries deemed it especially important to keep Britain at least somehow engaged in Continental Europe. Even more important, though, was their need to see Germany's economy restored—the Dutch in par-

3. As Karl Jaspers put it, in a letter to Hannah Arendt, "[Our] destiny today is that Germany can only exist in a united Europe, that the revival in her old glory can come about only through the unification of Europe, that the devil with whom we will inevitably have to make our pact is the egoistic, bourgeois society of the French."

ticular could not hope to revive and modernize their own economy unless they could sell to a growing German market. Even without Britain as a reassuring presence the Benelux countries needed a revived Germany and were willing to run the risk it entailed; so much so that for some Dutch politicians, like Foreign Minister Dirk Stikker, Germany was even a desirable counterweight to French economic domination.

Great Britain, meanwhile, continued to see the organization of postwar Europe in a quite different light. Sharing neither France's need for German raw materials, the Dutch desire for German markets, nor the Federal Republic's hunger for international recognition and acceptance, Britain could remain aloof, secure in its cultural, political, and economic links with the non-European world. It is fashionable today to attribute British abstention from Europe at the time to the unique British wartime experience, as one of only two victorious European combatants in the war against Hitler, and the only one never to have suffered occupation. Britain, it is thus contended, lacked the recent experience that led other Europeans to accept diminished sovereignty in return for economic and national revival. But that is at best a half-truth; the British certainly had no such recent memories of occupation or defeat and they continued for decades after the war to imagine that they could somehow go on as before. But the fact is that in 1950 very few Europeans, British or other, and none in positions of power, were talking about "giving up sovereignty."

The European entity that began to emerge in the 1950s was thus, in certain vital respects, an accident. It was neither predicted nor predictable—in either its form or its membership. In September 1947 George Kennan had concluded that the Europeans were so lacking in any capacity for collective vision or agreement that the State Department would have to "decide unilaterally" what was good for them. He was not mistaken at the time: in June 1948 it was by just four votes that the French National Assembly agreed to approve the establishment of a federal German authority in the three (French, British, American) western zones of occupied Germany.

Moreover, the coming of the ECSC did not in itself signify a strong or secure European consciousness even among its partners. As some commentators have noted, the Schuman Plan, signed into life on April 18, 1951, was really a sort of de facto peace treaty between France and West Germany, institutionalizing an important but restricted mutual economic interdependence and not much more. Once the European Recovery Program—the Marshall Plan—came to an end (proposed in 1947, it began the following year and was scheduled to phase out within four years) the limits of the Schuman Plan became obvious. The French blocked all further efforts at European integration: the so-called Green Pool to co-ordinate agricultural output, proposed by the Dutch in 1952 and buried with French encouragement three years later, and the plan for a European Defense Force, on which the French were divided (Gaullists and Communists against, the center parties favorable) and which was abandoned by the West Europeans after an adverse vote in the French Assembly in August 1954.

When the initiative was recovered, at the 1955 meeting in Messina, Sicily, of representatives of the Six, it was once again for largely circumstantial reasons. The economic boom of the times was pushing countries to find ways to stabilize trade in more than just coal and steel; the per capita GNP of the Federal Republic doubled during the fifties; Italy's exports to EEC countries alone almost doubled in the decade 1955–65. Such rates of economic expansion would have forced upon their European beneficiaries some sort of arrangements for its regulation, with or without the prior existence of the Coal and Steel Community. The 1957 agreement to establish a Common Market, like its predecessor of 1950, was the effect of new developments which it was designed to channel and contain, as well as a new device for addressing some very old problems.

This can best be understood by considering the way West Europeans addressed one particular problem, that of agriculture.[4] The Common Agricultural Policy, which kept European agricultural target prices above world

4. For much of what follows I am indebted to the stimulating discussion of agricultural protection in chapter 5 of Alan Mildward's *The European Rescue of the Nation-State* (Berkeley, Los Angeles, 1992).

prices, while guaranteeing to buy surpluses at predetermined rates, has long been the most expensive of the policies associated with the European Community—in the early 1970s it took up 70 percent of the EEC's budget. On the face of it, this was and is a monstrously irrational misapplication of resources: in 1980 agriculture employed just 14 percent of the labor force in Italy, 8.7 percent in France, and a mere 5.6 percent in the Federal Republic of Germany. Even in 1960 agriculture's share in the GNP of France was just 9 percent. Why, then, would the rest of Europe accede so readily to pressure, first applied by France in the mid-fifties and sustained ever since, to put a policy of agricultural protection and price-fixing at the heart of the construction of "Europe"?

The answer has very little to do with the present, and nothing at all to do with "Europe." Ever since the late nineteenth century, Europe, east and west alike, had suffered from rural overpopulation. Despite migration to the cities and emigration to North and South America, much of the European peasantry barely scraped a living from their labors. After the First World War the situation worsened, as the price of agricultural produce fell about three times as fast as that of nonagricultural goods. Democratic governments could do little to raise the price of agricultural products without angering their urban electorates, and in the economic circumstances of the interwar years they were in no position to invest heavily in agricultural support programs. Authoritarian regimes, in Spain, Portugal, Italy, and throughout eastern Europe, tried to impose policies designed to secure agricultural autarky, but these proved economically disastrous. High rates of urban unemployment precluded alternative occupation for underemployed or financially desperate farmers and farm workers. A depressed peasantry with voting powers turned everywhere to Fascist or populist parties promising to redress their grievances.

The shadow of this dilemma, and the fact that Europe's unhappy farmers, from Germany to Bulgaria, had proved so susceptible to the Fascist appeal before the war, was a major element in postwar political and economic thinking, something we nowadays tend to forget. It should also be recalled that in 1950 farmers were still a significant presence in Continental Europe: 25 percent of the labor force in West Germany, 30 percent in France, 43 percent in Italy. Moreover, in the immediate aftermath of war there was a chronic food shortage everywhere and an urgent need to reduce food imports so as to save precious foreign (dollar) currency. As late as 1949 only Great Britain, Scandinavia, and Switzerland had reached their prewar food production levels. The rest of Europe was still encouraging its peasants to stay on the land and produce as much as possible as fast as possible, with the help of wartime aid measures that were kept in place. Meanwhile reforms were passed in France, Italy, and elsewhere to improve the situation and to confirm the rights of tenant-farmers and laborers, who, it was hoped, could now be won over to democratic policies that would look to their interests.

Once the immediate postwar production crisis had been overcome, the nature of the agricultural problem shifted. By 1955, as in earlier decades, the issue was how to keep food prices up for farmers while holding them at a reasonable level for consumers. At the same time a boom in the production and trade of nonagricultural products was opening up an income gap between urban and rural workers that was troublingly reminiscent of the interwar years. And lastly, despite a steady fall in the number of people engaged in agriculture, the supply of food was now growing very fast, as new methods and greater efficiency increased productivity.

The result was the Common Market's Common Agricultural Policy (CAP). From the mid-1950s onward French governments of all political shades accepted the transnational aspects of the EEC that they would otherwise have found distasteful in return for "Europeanizing" their own policies of agricultural protection. For reasons of their own—largely to protect themselves against competition from Denmark—the Dutch went along. For the West Germans the CAP represented some domestic advantage, especially in the south, but was largely, once again, a price worth paying for the other benefits of an expanded trading community; besides, only in return for such a policy would France adopt common commercial policies, not to mention "ever-closer union," in the words of the preamble to the Treaty of Rome. The curious thing about the CAP is that it never benefited a majority of peasants, even in France. Working chiefly to the advantage of big grain and dairy producers, it offered much less to the growers and sellers of olives, vegetables, fruit, and wine.

The true function of the Common Agricultural Policy is thus political, not economic. In electoral terms, however, it was decreasingly relevant; the number of peasant voters in the states of the European Community fell steadily and sharply through the 1950s and 1960s, the decline only slowing down briefly with the adhesion of Spain, Portugal, and Greece twenty years later. If French politicians had merely been counting votes they could have saved themselves the trouble and expense of such a policy. But precisely because rural society was so swiftly melting away in a country where it had once been a dominant presence, there grew up a compensatory myth of its cultural centrality, a French version of the analogous German attachment to *Heimat*. Against the powerful belief that the rural community should be preserved and protected even as it was vanishing, demographic evidence and economic calculation counted for little. Combined with the memory of rural discontent from earlier decades, this sentiment has guaranteed the survival of a hugely costly European agricultural protection program into our own time, in utter contradiction to the general thrust of European economic policies and out of all proportion to the size of the constituency it purports to serve.

In certain respects this agricultural policy can stand as a metaphor illustrating the whole enterprise of "Europe." A fortuitous outcome of separate and distinctive electoral concerns, economic interests, and national political cultures, it was made necessary by circumstance and rendered possible by prosperity. Only after the fact has it been incorporated into a broader account of the coming together of European nations; had the latter project been the true initial objective, no such policy might ever have been attached to it in the first place.

Much the same may be said of each subsequent stage of joint European action. From 1951 to the 1957 signing of the Rome Treaty setting up a "common market" and on to 1968 (the establishment of a full customs union), from the 1969 Hague summit agreement to expand the Community through the 1985 Single European Act, from the 1991 Treaty of Maastricht formally declaring a "European Union" and beyond, the history of the formation of an "ever-closer union" has followed a consistent pattern: the real or apparent logic of mutual economic advantage not sufficing to account for the complexity of its formal arrangements, there has been invoked a sort of ontological ethic of political community; projected backward, the latter is then adduced to account for the gains made thus far and to justify further unificatory efforts. It is hard to resist recalling George

Santayana's definition of fanaticism: redoubling your efforts when you have forgotten your aim.

To question the European Union's increasingly grandiose and anachronistic account of its nature and purposes is not to dismiss its achievements. On the contrary. The astonishing recovery and subsequent prosperity of Western Europe, especially those parts of it joined in the Union, is in large measure attributable to various international agreements and arrangements which its members have made among themselves and which are chiefly responsible for their success in avoiding a repetition of the disasters of the interwar decades. This success is singular in modern European history: but that, as I shall argue, is just the point. Whatever made possible the Western Europe we now have was almost certainly unique—and unrepeatable. To suppose that it can be projected indefinitely into the future is an illusion, however worthy and well intentioned. To appreciate this, we need to look a little more closely at some of the circumstances of its emergence.

Four aspects of the European situation in the decade after Hitler's defeat contributed to the special context from which modern Western Europe grew. The first of these was quite simply the impact of the war itself. During the war belligerent and occupied states alike mobilized their resources and populations in unprecedented ways. The Germans invested heavily in their own war industries, some of which—notably in the metallurgical sector—survived the defeat surprisingly unscathed and went on to play an important part in the postwar economic revival. In some of the occupied countries, such as Belgium or Czechoslovakia, Germany's military presence, by simultaneously stimulating production and restraining labor protest, actually favored the accumulation of profits and gave a preliminary boost to postwar modernization. Everywhere the organization of society for war paved the way for a presumption that in peacetime there would be comparably high levels of state involvement in everything from social welfare to economic planning—in Michael Howard's words, "war and welfare went hand in hand."[5]

This presumption in favor of centralized economic and social organization, shared to a greater or lesser degree by all major political groupings in every European country, was a crucial factor in facilitating postwar reconstruction, domestic and international alike. In the words of one authority on economic planning, writing in 1949, "We are all planners now."[6] The very fact that all European states were now taking control of their economies made it easier to imagine pooling aspects of that control in a multinational authority, something that would have been unthinkable after World War I.

5. Michael Howard, *The Lessons of History* (London, 1987), p. 127.
6. See E.F.M. Durbin, *Problems of Economic Planning* (London, 1949).

The Second World War was peculiar both in that it had divided countries against themselves and in that almost every European participant *lost*. It thus had the interesting and lasting consequence of giving the sub-Continent something else in common: a shared recent memory of war, civil war, occupation, and defeat. Despite the huge human losses of the First World War the sense of a common experience of conflict and destruction was far greater after 1945. As a result, Europeans became, collectively, "defeatist"—not only unwilling to fight one another anymore but wary of any commitment to fighting at all.

This was not very surprising: Austria had, by 1945, lost six wars in succession since the time of Metternich; France had suffered three costly and debilitating continental wars in the span of one man's lifetime, from each of which the country emerged poorer and weaker. Belgium had been fought over and occupied twice in thirty years. It is significant that ever since 1945 opinion polls across Western Europe show a consistent reluctance on the part of most people to express any confidence in their own state's military capacity, little support for high military expenditure, and no sustained inclination to treat military prowess as a measure of national greatness. The two outstanding exceptions to this pattern are Great Britain and Finland—the only two west European states to have emerged from the Second World War with a creditable military record of which to boast.

The shared experience of defeat points to another

common European wartime experience: the memory of things best forgotten (here, too, the British and the Finns were fortunate exceptions). Günter Grass has pointed out the ironic advantage that Germany enjoyed after 1945: with nothing to be proud of in their recent past, and a cultural and political heritage in ashes, Germans could repress unpleasant memories and concentrate on rebuilding from zero. It is an observation with some pertinence for Germany's victims as well. In spite or perhaps because of deliberately overblown myths of collective resistance to domestic and foreign oppression, the French, the Italians, and the Dutch in particular had equally good reason to put recent history behind them and start from scratch; past emphases on national and military achievements appeared somehow inappropriate and were suppressed, with attention turned instead above all to social and economic affairs.

Hitler's lasting gift to Europe was thus the degree to which he and his collaborators made it impossible henceforth to dwell with comfort upon the past. The contrast with sentiment after the First World War is striking here: after 1918 the mood of exhaustion was accompanied by a widespread desire to recapture, somehow, the certainties and the security of the prewar years. No such nostalgia could be found in Europe following the end of the Second World War.

The second element in the postwar situation that facilitated the construction of "Europe" was the Cold War. From 1947 onward it was clear to most European leaders that the Soviet Union posed a serious threat to eastern Europe and that even if only for their own protection the states of western Europe must come into some form of alliance with one another and with the United States. Great Britain, and in particular the British Foreign Secretary from 1945 to 1951, Ernest Bevin, saw this first, France last; but no one in western Europe except a few intellectuals seriously believed that a third path, between the U.S.S.R. and a Western Alliance, was open to them. In February 1948 the Communist Party in Czechoslovakia engineered a bloodless coup, seizing power in the only remaining eastern or east-central European country not already under effective Soviet control. Together with the simultaneous increase in Communist-led social protest in France and Italy, the shock of the Prague coup further concentrated the minds of West European leaders, and helped to overcome long-standing European resentment of American power and suspicion of the motives of U.S. foreign policy.

One possible consequence of the renewed fear of war might well have been the need to rearm at a time when Western Europe had hardly begun its economic recovery. This would have been both economically and politically disastrous (the relatively mild recession brought on by increased military spending during the Korean War is an indication of what might have been). But the huge U.S. commitment to Europe, in the form of an increased U.S. military presence and direct economic aid via the Marshall Plan, helped the Western Europeans to square the circle: the Cold War forced them into a greater measure of unity and collaboration while sparing them attendant military expenses. Instead, as they got ever richer, so the relative burden of defense spending in their budgets fell dramatically. In 1953 it represented 11 percent of the GNP of France and Britain, just under 5 percent in Italy and the Federal Republic. By 1970 it was 5 percent in Britain, 4 percent in France, and around 3 percent in West Germany and Italy.[7]

The breakup of the wartime alliance of the United States, Great Britain, and the Soviet Union and the creation within Europe of two hostile blocs also helps to account for a development that would otherwise have been inconceivable: the rapid and uncontentious absorption of (western) Germany into the West European family. The British could not afford to pay the costs of occupying their own devastated zone of Germany; the United States wanted a wealthy and loyal German state to play a role in the Western Alliance; as a result the

---

7. Looking back from a post-1989 vantage point, and from a typically anti-American stance, a former French foreign minister acknowledged the point: "Rangée dans un camp, en étroite tutelle des Etats-Unis, reçevant ses instructions et venant au rapport, elle [Europe] s'était rassurée de tout, à force d'être irresponsable. Aujourd'hui, elle commence à regretter ce bon temps du sans-souci." ["Lined up in one camp, under strict U.S. control, taking orders and reporting for duty, Europe was reassured but at a cost of irresponsibility. Today it is starting to regret those carefree times."] Michel Jobert, in *Le Monde*, August 10, 1991.

mistakes of 1919 were miraculously avoided—even though after 1945 there were altogether more convincing grounds than after the war of 1914–18 for treating Germany as a pariah state, guilty of crimes of war that the poor Kaiser had never imagined. Thanks to the Cold War the Germans on both sides of the divide were reincorporated into their respective Europes on remarkably non-discriminatory terms.[8]

If the war and the Cold War facilitated the postwar political strategies of European statesmen, it was the disastrous recent economic history of the continent that gave a special quality to the ensuing boom. European economic progress in the first half of the twentieth century had been triply delayed or distorted: by the First World War, by the stagnation and misconceived policies of the interwar years, and then by the war that followed. The benefits of Nazi war-related investment in no way compensated for the destruction wrought by the weaponry thereby manufactured. As a result of the Malthu-

8. The Morgenthau Plan, named after Henry Morgenthau, Jr., U.S. Secretary of the Treasury, which envisaged the "pastoralization" of postwar Germany, was never seriously considered by U.S. foreign-policy makers. Certainly there were debates, in the United States as within West Germany itself, on the form of a new German state as well as on the question of de-Nazification of its political elite. But the Cold War effectively foreclosed alternative strategies and gave primacy to the need for a reliable and friendly German ally in the coming struggle with the U.S.S.R.

sian practices of commerce and industry between the wars, the lost opportunities for investment and modernization, and the destruction of plant and transportation infrastructure, Western Europe after 1945 was catching up not just to 1939, 1929, or even 1918 but to 1913. In France, to take just one example, the average age of industrial equipment at the liberation was twenty-five years.

This huge lag to be made up was at once a burden and an opportunity. That it was indeed seized as an opportunity is of course to the credit of economic administrators and planners—men like Robert Marjolin, who worked with Jean Monnet on the French postwar Plan before moving on to high office in the European Community; postwar civil servants and economic advisers such as Marjolin had been frustratedly awaiting their chance ever since the onset of the Depression. The speed of the recovery was especially marked in the Federal Republic of Germany, where it mattered most, since the rest of the West European economy depended upon it. By the last quarter of 1949 the western sectors of Germany had regained their 1936 output level, only to pass it by 30 percent a year later.

Even more tellingly, the Federal Republic had a positive balance of trade with the rest of Western Europe in 1949 by the export of raw materials, notably coal. A year later its trade balance was in deficit—it was already consuming its own raw materials. By 1951 West Germany had begun the first of the huge trade surpluses that marked its economic performance thereafter—but now in manufactured commodities. And as Germany went, so, in time, went its partners.

The economic "miracle" was accompanied and made possible in Western Europe by social and economic reforms, which had also been postponed for a generation or more. Before the war (male) peasants and workers had had the vote but little else, which goes a long way to accounting for the polarized political history of the 1930s. After 1945 there were improvements in tenants' rights, the institution of state-guaranteed pensions, medical and accident insurance, trade-union rights, paid vacations, and good-quality subsidized housing; Western Europe began the long process of catching up in the field of social and welfare rights the ground already covered in the political and legal reforms of the previous century. Most of the results were not evident until the mid-1950s, at about the point when the sub-Continent was assured of the means to pay for them. But the reward was a long and once again unprecedented era of relative social peace and political stability.

Lastly, and in close connection with these interrelated social changes and economic modernization, Western Europe experienced a second and final agrarian revolution. It has been estimated that in West Germany a unit of farm labor that in 1900 would have fed five people in 1950 fed six. In other words, there had been virtually no increase in agricultural productivity in the first half of the twentieth century. But by 1980 the same unit of labor could feed *thirty-five* persons. The implications of this transformation were enormous—and would have been greater still had Western Europeans not chosen to overcharge themselves for food in order to sustain a shrinking peasant sector. As it was, whereas most Western Europeans spent half or more of their income on food, drink, and tobacco before 1945 (only the Dutch and the Scandinavians spent less), by 1980 they were spending a quarter or less, and living better.

These were unrepeatable, one-time transformations. That is to say, Western Europe will probably never again have to catch up on thirty years of economic stagnation or half a century of agrarian depression, or rebuild after a disastrous war. Nor will it be bound together by the need to do so, or by the coincidence of Communist threat and American encouragement. For good and ill the postwar circumstances, the midwife of mid-twentieth-century Western European prosperity, were unique; no one else will have the same good fortune.

Just how far did this transformation of Western Europe in the decades after the war alter its standing in the world? Certainly, a failure to reconstruct Europe in these years would have been disastrous; in 1946 there was little confidence in the prospect. Janet Flanner, admittedly a rather capricious observer, wrote in October of that year that Europeans were "slowly entering a new ice age."[9] But what exactly *was* achieved as a result of the recovery of confidence and the economic renewal that ensued? As we have seen, there was a huge and sustained increase in *intra*-European trade; i.e., the Western Europeans contributed to their own prosperity by selling goods to one another. But this simply put Western Europeans back to where they had been in 1913, when some 60 percent of European countries' commerce was with one another. If anything, the interdependence of European trade and capital flows in the years 1850–1913 was probably greater than that achieved by the European Economic Community, at least until very recently.

What is more, and despite the contribution of Marshall Aid, GATT, OECD, EFTA, and the EEC itself, the West European economies did not regain 1913 levels of import and export (as a percentage of GNP) until the mid-1970s. Until then they were simply making up for the cataclysmic collapse in trade of the years in between. As for Western Europe's contribution to *world* exports of manufactured goods, we should not be surprised to note that Great Britain's share fell from 22.4 percent in 1929 to just 9.7 percent in 1980. This, after all, is said to be one of the penalties the U.K. paid for failing to join the European club. But France, whose

---

9. Three years later, in the summer of 1949, she reported that the same Europe was "a great, pleasurable, money-making and money-spending touring ground." She was wrong in both cases.

share of worldwide manufactured goods exports was 10.9 percent in 1929, had climbed back to 10 percent by 1980. The figures for West Germany are comparable: 20.5 percent in 1929, 19.9 percent in 1980 (by contrast, the Japanese share of the same index rose nearly 400 percent in the same years). It seems fair to conclude that among European states, what distinguished EEC countries from others was that the former were enabled, slowly, to recover lost ground, whereas the latter never did.

By such measures the outstanding accomplishment of the European Community was to put its members back, more or less, where they had once been. In the circumstances this was no mean achievement, but its significance should not be misread. If Western Europe in the years of its fastest growth and greatest prosperity was only playing catch-up, then its long-term prospects in an era of slower growth are unpromising. Moreover, a price was paid for the rapid economic changes and the overwhelming importance attached to them. In all the major West European nations, and in spite of the age of stability and prosperity through which they were passing, there was a common undercurrent of disappointment; a sense that the promise and opportunity of the immediate postwar years was somehow wasted.

The form of that disappointment varied by country. In France and in Italy the political coalitions that had emerged from the wartime resistance movements squabbled and split, squandering their capital of goodwill and radical promise. In Italy this led to a monopoly of power by the Christian Democratic Party and a growing public disillusion with the practices of democratic politics. In France the high hopes of the postwar era were lost in the frustrations of parliamentary politicking and personal score-settling; in the words of Albert Camus, the dream of moral revolution, of reconstructing postwar France, had not only failed but "had fallen into disrepute." As a result, highly creditable economic performance was accompanied by chronic political instability and a growing sense of institutionalized corruption and public disillusion.

In Britain the 1945 victory of Attlee's Labour Party and the accompanying expectations of a "New Jerusalem" came and went. Much was achieved, notably in health and education; but much, too, was neglected—in the infrastructure of public equipment (transportation, roads, housing, and services) and in the field of economic and urban planning; in a sense Victorian Britain lingered on into the mid-1950s, only to be replaced in short order by "swinging London." In West Germany a deliberately blinkered concentration on economic reconstruction, with its morally anesthetizing effect on public life, was summarized unforgivably well by the leader of the Bavarian Christian Social Union, Franz Josef Strauss, in 1969: "A people who have achieved such economic performances," he informed his audience, "have the right not to have to hear any more about Auschwitz."

Rather than "hear any more about Auschwitz," Western Europe and its official spokesmen gave themselves over to the worship of their own economic achievements. In 1960 the OECD forecast an indefinite future of continuing and even increasing rates of growth. A decade later its prognostications were a little more modest, but still promised annual growth rates averaging 5 percent or more "in the medium term." Most tellingly of all, the authors of the Single European Act, the 1985 agreement to proceed with all due speed toward a single market and the dismantling of internal barriers within the European Community, could still invoke "growth" as the common objective and binding ideology of a future, integrated Europe. Western Europeans were being invited to inhabit the imagined world of Saint-Simon—a society of *industriels* for whom the production and distribution of wealth were the only common faith.

The great European economic boom and its illusions were the product of special postwar circumstances. Among these should also be counted the Marshall Plan, a coincidence of great American wealth and the Truman Administration's willingness to spend it on a program of credits, grants, and gifts to Europe. Marshall Plan aid itself amounted to some $13 billion over the years 1948–52, part of an overall program of U.S. support for Europe in the decade after 1945 that totaled $24.8 billion (of which the U.K. got $6.9 billion, France $5.5 billion, the Federal Republic $3.9 billion, and Italy $2.9 billion).

There is disagreement over the precise economic significance of this assistance to Western Europe—some scholars have argued that Europe would have "taken off" anyway, but more slowly; the European economic crisis of 1947, the continent's inability to pay for its vital primary imports that triggered the Marshall program, is seen by such analysts as a crisis of growth: an expanding demand for raw materials encountering a shortage of dollars with which to buy them. What seems more to the point is that the economic recovery, requiring as it did that European governments make hard choices—e.g., between investing in modernization and consumption—would almost certainly have been accompanied by far more political and social turmoil had American aid not eased the way. As it was, the Marshall Plan put Western Europe in the uniquely fortunate situation of being able to import primary materials, invest in public infrastructure, and maintain and increase earnings and domestic consumption, all the while holding unemployment down to historically low levels and even keeping inflation under control.

Two other factors contributed to Western Europe's apparent success in vanquishing the historical cycle of crises hitherto believed to be endemic to capitalist economies. An acute shortage of workers, at least until the mid-1960s, when the first generation of baby boomers entered the labor force, was easily overcome by the importation of cheap, docile foreign labor: from British, French, and Dutch colonies, from Mediterranean Europe, and, in the northern Italian case, from its own under-developed southern periphery. West Germany had the further benefit of more than 10 million refugees—from East Prussia, Poland, Czechoslavakia, Yugoslavia, and other countries and regions where Germans had once lived for centuries and whence they were now expelled following the liberation. The burden of supporting these refugees—and feeding their political fantasies of impending revenge—was more than offset by the additional skills and strength they brought to a country whose growing economy could absorb all the labor power available to it.

That postwar Western Europe needed labor so badly and could absorb it so unproblematically is a reminder that until the 1960s its economy, like so much else about the continent, was still recognizably heir to the industrial societies of the previous century. The best illustration of this is also the third major factor in the economic takeoff of the period: coal. Before the war, coal accounted for 90 percent of all industrial and domestic energy consumption in France, Germany, the United Kingdom, and the Benelux countries. Five years after the war, in 1950, it still met 82 percent of the *primary* energy consumption of the six ECSC countries (France, Italy, West Germany, Netherlands, Belgium, and Luxembourg). Agreement on the production and distribution of this vital commodity thus lay at the heart of any revival of the continent's productive capacities. Coal was *the* European resource, locally available and relatively cheap to produce (the initial investment having been made many years before). In Europe of the 1950s steel was fired with coal; trains that transported coal from mines to furnaces, from pitheads to hearths, were propelled by coal-burning engines; the vast majority of households used coal for heat if no longer for cooking; and the major West European cities, starting with London, were covered by a permanent haze of coal dust, always liable to transform itself into a choking smog. The men who produced this precious resource were still the proud aristocracy of a traditional labor force.

By 1960 Western Europe's industrial dependence on coal had fallen to just 48 percent, and it dropped further still in the coming decade. But in the first fifteen years after the war Europe was spared the political and economic upheavals that ensued from this dramatic change; more to the point, without the vital role that coal had always played, and was expected to continue to play, in the domestic economies of the time, the shared interest of the West European states in forming an international economic community might have been much less obvious. The advantageous coincidence of a common political outlook notwithstanding—all six of the foreign ministers who signed the original ECSC Treaty were Christian Democrats—it was domestic economic problems, for the solving of which an international agreement over the trade in coal and steel was taken to be essential, that drove the European enterprise forward.

But more even than coal, labor, and dollars, sheer good fortune fueled the vehicle of European unity: the fact that five of Europe's actually or potentially wealthiest countries were among its six founding members; the convenience of waiting until 1973 before absorbing a further three and until the 1980s before being constrained to make room for the poorer lands of Mediterranean Europe; most of all, the peculiar advantage of never having to worry, from 1951 to 1989, about the implications of trying to incorporate into "Europe" even poorer lands to the east. This was indeed luck, and not choice, or at least not official policy. On the contrary, from the outset part of what made *this* European trade partnership different from all previous attempts was that it professed all manner of expansionist future intentions. Far from confining itself to protecting the interests of its present members, the European Community and its successor entities claimed that these could best be ensured by extending to others their own rules and benefits.

*This* is the foundation myth of modern Europe—that the European Community was and remains the kernel of a greater, pan-European prospect. Without such a myth, all the means by which this "Europe" came into being—the Marshall Plan, ECSC, economic planning, OECD, common agricultural policies, and the like, even the European Court—would be merely so many practical solutions to particular problems. As it was, they were the necessary conditions for the remaking of Europe, but in themselves insufficient. The otherwise self-sufficient, self-satisfied, even selfish "Europe" centered in Brussels became a beacon for the rest of the continent and a source of respect and credibility for itself because of the promise that *this* Europe was no Zollverein, no mere neo-mercantilist partnership of the rich and famous, no temporary practical and empirical solution to daily economic dilemmas. *This* Europe was the Europe of all Europeans—even if there were practical political impediments to their immediate membership of it. In the case of Great Britain, or Spain, such impediments could be overcome and therefore would be, in order for the principles of the organism to remain in good standing (though not without much internal wrangling and enduring regret among the administrators of some of the original six member nations). But other nations seemed to be definitively excluded for the foreseeable future.

This was, of course, a source of official distress in communiqués from Brussels and at meetings of the heads of the Western European states. But for forty years after 1949 the Western Europeans got on with the business of rebuilding their quadrant of the continent, secure in the knowledge not only that the U.S. defense budget would protect them against external threat but that the self-interest of the U.S.S.R., in turn, would protect them against the risk of unwanted expansion. In short, the Western Europeans came to have a strong and growing interest in keeping Europe divided. Only the West Germans came close to acknowledging this, in the *Ostpolitik* of Willy Brandt and his Social Democratic successors, whereby improvements in West–East relations after 1969 were bought (literally bought in the case of favors paid to the German Democratic Republic) by recognition of the Communist regimes in Eastern Europe and "understanding" of their needs and interests. Public protestations to the contrary notwithstanding, the European Community of the 1970s and 1980s not only presumed the permanence of Europe's division but depended upon it. The more secure that division, the easier it was to imagine a closer and more prosperous union of nations to the west of the line—while at the same time holding out the illusory prospect of that union's hypothetical expansion to the east "one day."

Thus when the news reached western capitals of the fall of the Berlin Wall and the ensuing collapse of Communist regimes, official pleasure was followed with some alacrity by the expression of doubt. It was not by chance that the French President François Mitterrand speculated a little too openly, at the time of the abortive coup against Mikhail Gorbachev in August 1991, that some form of Soviet government might yet survive in Moscow, just as he and other French diplomats strove helplessly first to prevent German unification, then to discourage the Czech Republic and other Eastern European states from presenting themselves as candidates for "European" membership.[10] More than most, France —the major initiator and beneficiary of postwar West European international arrangements—had good reason to know that the illusion of Europe would not survive being put to a continent-wide test. As Freud observed in *Civilization and Its Discontents* concerning the conditions for human affection: "It is always possible to bind together a considerable number of people in love, so long as there are other people left over to receive the manifestations of their aggressiveness."

10. In March 1993, Jacek Kuroń, former leader of Solidarity and a strong Polish advocate of a liberal, democratic, "European" Poland, wrote in *Polytyka* that he had begun to detect among West European political figures a nostalgia for the old world and for the U.S.S.R. His only mistake lay in supposing that this nostalgia was new.

## 2

# EASTERN APPROACHES

HOW MANY Europes are there? The question sounds odd, and one answer may seem intuitively obvious. There is only one Europe, just as there is but one Asia, one Africa, and so forth. Like the other continents, Europe has a north and a south, an east and a west, and appropriate subdivisions within these. True, the eastern boundaries of the European continent are fuzzy, shading into western Asia across a broad and topographically indefinite terrain; but elsewhere its limits are clear enough. Moreover Europe is a small continent with a long history of self-awareness, which means that to be a European is to have an identity rather more precise than that attaching to persons who are "African" or "Asian" or "American" by virtue of their geographical origin. Notwithstanding occasional attempts at constructing a "pan-African" consciousness, the peoples of Africa, for example, are united by very little more than a common experience of colonialism. "Europeanness" by contrast, is something the peoples of Europe have brought upon themselves. Between their geographical contiguity and their common past they do seem to share something indigenous and fundamental.

Curiously, though, one of the things that Europeans have long shared and that has bound them together is a sense of their divisions. Indeed, drawing distinctions among and between themselves has been one of the defining obsessions of the inhabitants of the continent. The breakup of the original Roman Empire into two distinct parts at the end of the fourth century A.D. began this process, whereby a single entity was defined by its very bifurcation; the emergence of the Carolingian monarchy reinforced the point by giving the western part of Europe, hitherto anarchic and administratively imprecise, distinctive and enduring frontiers. Charlemagne's ninth-century empire corresponded with curious anticipatory precision to the original postwar "Europe" of the Six—France, West Germany, the Benelux countries, and Italy, though it left out central and southern Italy and included present-day Catalonia. The Roman, Carolingian, and some later empires lacked precise borders, petering out instead in *limes*, marches, and military zones; and the eastern edges of the Carolingian monarchy, like the northern boundaries of Byzantium, were always imprecise. But by the fourteenth century, when the European frontier "closed," the east–west distinction in Europe was remarkably well established.

It is sometimes supposed, today, that the line dividing eastern from western Europe was an artificial creation of the Cold War, an iron curtain gratuitously and recently drawn across a single cultural space. This is not so. In the nineteenth century, long after the Habsburg rulers had established effective authority over territories stretching well into today's Ukraine, the Austrian Chancellor Metternich could famously speak of Asia as beginning at the *Landstrasse*, the road leading east out of Vienna. Nor was his an original observation: the Englishman Edward Brown, who traveled through the Habsburg lands in 1669, remarked that upon entering Hungary "a man seems to take leave of our world . . . and, before he cometh to Buda, seems to enter upon a new stage of world, quite different from that of the Western countrys."[1] Whatever the sources of their prejudice, both the Austrian and the Englishman were noting, and confirming, an invisible line that already ran from north to south through the middle of Europe. Conradus Celtis, a German writer of the late fifteenth century, recorded strikingly familiar resentments: "*Our* famous harbour, Danzig," he wrote, "is held by the Pole, and the gateway of *our* ocean, The Sound, by the Dane." Not content with anticipating by more than three centuries one source of contemporary European conflict, Celtis then went on to complain about another: to the east were communities "separated from the body of our Germany . . . like the Transylvanian Saxons who also use our racial culture and speak our native language."[2]

1. Larry Wolff, *Inventing Eastern Europe: The Map of Civilization on the Mind of the Enlightenment* (Stanford, 1994), p. 41.
2. See N.J.G. Pounds, *An Historical Geography of Europe* (Cambridge, 1990), where Celtis is quoted on page 215.

Like Adam of Bremen, an eleventh-century chronicler who noted that "Slavia" began east of the Elbe and ran south to the Black Sea, Celtis and his successors were recording a sentiment that has been repeated on many occasions in western Europe ever since the end of the tenth century: where the Roman/Carolingian/Lotharingian/Hohenzollern/Habsburg empire(s) ended, there ended Europe. And since the only major population movement within Europe after the (ninth century A.D.) arrival of the Magyars in the Danubian plain consisted of German settlers moving eastward, the natural inclination of (western) Europeans was to think of the eastern lands as somehow *terra incognita*, composed of rough peoples awaiting civilization and government. Long after those same peoples had come under the sway of imperial authorities to the west and east, something of the same attitude remained.

Reinforcing this ancient division was a religious one. All the European empires, beginning with the late Roman one, were closely identified with a dominant religion. Byzantium imposed Orthodox Christianity upon the territories it controlled, just as Charlemagne enforced the Roman version in his lands. Later, their Russian and Austrian heirs did likewise, though only the eastern empires over time associated and even conflated temporal and spiritual power. As a consequence, these two forms of Christianity came to define different regions of Europe. Indeed, in many ways the ecclesiastical boundaries and practices of the distant past are the most enduring of all European divisions—the dioceses through which the Catholic Church in France is administered today draw on the geographical subdivisions of Roman provincial organization; the Ottoman frontier in the Balkans and the practice of millet (the accordance of privileges to Christians under Turkish rule in return for services, notably military service) is all too well reflected in the salience of Orthodox Christianity as an identifying tag in that region. In areas of mixed population, religious affiliation also expressed and conferred social standing: in the Baltic region, landowners were Catholic, peasants Orthodox. And these socioreligious distinctions were further echoed in language use. Just as Jews were distinguished by speaking Yiddish, so Orthodox peasants in the territory of present-day Poland and Ukraine spoke Lithuanian, Ruthenian, or some other local language or dialect, while Catholics in the same district spoke Polish. By the nineteenth century the emergence of "national" identities in the Habsburg lands especially was often a matter of language, even if the language in question was by no means ancient and had even been (re)invented for political ends; the adoption of one among a number of Croatian or Slovakian dialects to represent a "national" language for a future state may not have been wholly random, but it was without question arbitrary.

Within western Europe the salient division was not east–west but north–south. By the seventeenth century this distinction was quite pronounced: northern Europeans were characteristically Protestant (Lutheran, Calvinist, or Anglican), spoke a language with its roots in German, and were becoming divided into nation-states with clearly defined borders. Southern Europeans spoke a Latin-based language, practiced the Roman Catholic religion, and lived in communities still ruled over by emperors or popes. But these differences, which matter so much in the internal history of France and Germany, or in the history of conflicts among west European rulers, never acquired the significance of the division between west and east. This was because from the very beginning of its modern history, western Europe was bound by cultural and commercial links that transcended its internal divisions; from the twelfth-century urban renaissance to the eighteenth-century Enlightenment, the history of the western part of Europe was a common and distinctive history.

Certainly, the centers of economic and cultural gravity moved around quite dramatically—from the Rhineland to Lombardy, thence to Venetia, Tuscany, and back to the Low Countries, only to settle finally in the capitals of the great imperial states of the Atlantic fringe: Spain, France, and Britain. But they rarely moved very far east, and never beyond Vienna. Whatever the passing brilliance of the civilizations of Prague or Vilna, they were never capitals of something definably *European* in the way that was at different moments true of Florence, Madrid, Amsterdam, Paris, London, or Vienna. Why this should have been so is another question. The rise of the

Ottoman Turks and the discovery of the Americas shifted the center of gravity of European history dramatically toward the Atlantic. The Counter-Reformation and the military defeat of the Protestant aristocracy of Bohemia at the Battle of the White Mountain in 1620 were undoubtedly a historical disaster for Bohemia, coming as they did in the aftermath of a flourishing of learning and the arts in sixteenth-century Prague. The rise of Muscovy ended the reality (though not the enduring illusion) of Poland's central place in European history. But these things happened, and as a result much of what we have come to think of as the history of Europe is the history of *western* Europe, north and south alike.

If there is a distinctive western Europe, with northern and southern components, and a no less distinctive if less fortunate eastern Europe, where do they meet? On the ancient line running from Trieste to Gdansk/ Danzig? Is it enough to note the remarkable continuity between the outer limits of the Carolingian monarchy, the frontier between (some of the) Austrian and Hungarian territories in the Habsburg Empire, and the western edge of "real existing socialism" after 1947 in order to conclude that *tertium non datur*? It is true that from the Dalmatian coast to Lithuania there is a line dotted with fortresses, frontier settlements, strategic towns, historic crossroads, and the like, and for centuries it has been the point of encounter of Germans and Slavs, Austrians and Turks, Catholics and Orthodox. But it falls across a terrain where Poles, Lithuanians, and Russians

have also met, mixed, and fought. Roman Catholicism
stretches a good way farther east than Gdansk/Danzig,
German is (or was) spoken in towns and valleys far into
the Slavic heartlands, and Bohemia was an integral and
(until 1948) flourishing component in the Industrial
Revolution which more than anything else marked western Europe off from the rest of the continent. Would it
not be easier, as so many have suggested, to acknowledge
a further subdivision, that of *central* Europe?

There are many advantages to doing so. The quadri-
lateral bounded by lines running from, say, Riga to
Prague, on to Trieste and Zagreb, and back to the Baltic via Lvov has much in common. It is overwhelming-
ly Catholic, rural, and Slav-speaking, has experienced
similarly the impact of empire and the appeal of nationalism, and is dotted with towns and cities whose archi-
tectural heritage and literary traditions are unmistakably
those of mainstream Europe while displaying distinctive
traits and traditions of their own. For the century following 1848 its culture was much shaped by the presence of an influential intelligentsia, notably in the cities.
Most of all, it is markedly different from the lands to
its immediate east and south, and for centuries has
sought to maintain a distance from them. For good reasons of their own, therefore, the "central" Europeans of
this area place much emphasis upon the ancient division
between the Western and Eastern Roman empires,
which leaves them well within the western one.

But the problem with the idea of "central" Europe is

that it is a distinctively *modern* one, and it has no deep roots in Europe's past. It could not have come into existence until the political and economic reforms initiated by the later enlightened despots, notably Joseph II of Austria during the decade of the 1780s, and it was all but destroyed by the Versailles settlement and the national divisions to which the latter gave its imprimatur. Hitler did little more than administer the death blow. The only golden past to which "central" Europe can now refer is that of the last decades of the Habsburg Empire, when Prague and Budapest flourished as never before or since, and provincial towns like Lvov and Zagreb basked in the reflected glow of late imperial glory. To the rest of the world, however, and notably to west European observers, the distinction between central and eastern Europe before 1848 or after 1945 was by no means clear. We have already seen that to a seventeenth-century traveler Budapest was decidedly non-western, and few visitors from the west saw much to distinguish the buffer regions of Europe's center from the exotic lands to their east.

There certainly *were* differences, of course, and they are still visible today. The marshy terrain of eastern Poland, where Orthodoxy begins and a related language is written in a different alphabet, has little in common with Kraków, a sophisticated center of Catholic and secular learning much influenced by the experience of Habsburg government from Vienna; the same distinction holds between the highlands of Montenegro and the

German-speaking intelligentsia of Ljubljana (Laibach). But in both cases these disparate regions have on occasion formed parts of the same state. It would be fair to object that the real distinction here is not west/east but urban/rural, and that if "Central Europe" exists it is but the civilization of the cities of Habsburgia. Still, the fact remains that in Belorussia and Ukraine, in Romania, Bulgaria, Serbia, and even Greece, there is another world to which Prague and Budapest assuredly do not belong.

Yet the very distinction that confers their modern significance upon cities like Prague or Warsaw, Budapest or Zagreb—that they are the capitals of independent countries—has also deprived them of a claim to a place in the "center" of Europe. For their culture was a cosmopolitan culture, often written or spoken in an international language—German—many of whose most accomplished representatives were Jews. The destruction of this genuinely central European culture has left Polish Warsaw, Lithuanian Vilnius, Czech Prague, and Hungarian Budapest as provincial as Austrian Vienna. They may be located in the middle of Europe, but their claim to a distinctive "central Europeanness" is at best nostalgic, at worst bogus. Their desire to avoid being confused with places and peoples to their east is real enough and has deep historical roots—as "frontier" peoples athwart the historical crossroads of a continent, they have particular reason to try to avoid finding themselves on the wrong side of an important divide. But it does not follow from this that they can claim a distinctive identity, past or present, that guarantees them a permanent place on the "good" (and safe) side of such a line.

It may be more helpful to conceive of Europe as divided not geographically but in other ways.[3] There is and has always been a rich Europe and a poor one, but the frontier dividing them has shifted over the centuries. Not so long ago the Mediterranean littoral and its urban hinterland from Marseilles to Istanbul were among the most prosperous regions in Europe. By contrast the Scandinavian lands were poor for much of their recorded history. With notable exceptions, the reverse is true today. Cities were not always, as they are now, the site of extremes of wealth and poverty—if anything, that was the distinguishing characteristic of rural society, which is another reason why the largely rural eastern and southeastern parts of Europe fell so far behind the more urbanized northwest; the great urban corridor of Europe from Hamburg to Milan has always been a pole of prosperity and advantage.

And then there was the contrast between peoples with a state and those without. This is of course a political

3. Geography, after all, can confuse as well as enlighten. Since 1989 the "center of Europe" has been variously placed in a Polish marketplace, a Lithuanian field, a French farmhouse, and, most recently, a Belgian village, depending on the definition of the Europe in question. None of these four claimants would be anyone's intuitive choice for the continent's true midpoint.

distinction, but it is more than that. To have been formed into a recognized nation and a permanent state in earlier centuries was to have been extraordinarily fortunate; it is one of the ways in which the history of the Netherlands, of Sweden, of Britain, France, and even Spain is crucially different from that of Czechs, Poles, Croats, and many others. Whereas the northern and western European peoples formed states by expansion from a core, absorbing their own peripheries until constrained by topography or competition, the countries of modern eastern Europe were born and could only be born from the collapse of empires—Russian, Turkish, Austrian, German—a process that is still incomplete. Thus not only do they not have the advantage of coming first but their identity necessarily consists of an all-or-nothing claim to territory and power at the expense of a neighbor making an identical claim—in many cases over the same land. This is *the* great misfortune of the eastern half of Europe: that its division into states came late and all at once. It is what gives to these lands their common history and their common weakness—and it is what in the end makes them crucially different from the luckier peoples to their west.[4]

4. Germany and Italy may seem contradictory cases here—west European countries that united late but nonetheless overcame the disadvantage. It was by no means clear, however, until very recently indeed, that they would in fact survive the circumstances of their birth. But both comprised regions of great and ancient wealth; it also mattered that Italy and most

Moreover—and here, too, history and geography have conspired cruelly—Europe's eastern half consisted of many small peoples and states overshadowed by two great powers, the residue of empires, to their east and west alike. It still does. No comparable misfortune attended the birth of the independent states of western Europe; the Netherlands and Sweden emerged as independent territorial entities in the sixteenth and seventeenth centuries, after the decline of the medieval empires but before the rise of the modern great powers. The resulting differences are striking in many ways. The languages of the larger western nation-states became dominant international languages; their cultural references became those of Europe as a whole. Established, smaller western states like the Netherlands or Denmark could afford to recognize and share in this international culture, even make it their own, without running the risk of losing their own identity in the process.

But from the outset eastern or "central" Europeans, whose identity consisted largely in a series of negatives —not Russian, not Orthodox, not Turkish, not German, not Hungarian, and so forth—had provinciality forced upon them as an act of state-making. Their elites were obliged to choose between cosmopolitan allegiance to an extraterritorial unit or idea—the Church, an empire,

---

of Germany fell within the western division of the continent after the war. In the case of Italy especially, matters might have been otherwise.

Communism, or, most recently, "Europe"—or else the constricting horizon of nationalism and local interest. The option of being at once a citizen of one's own state and at the same time a free and equal participant in the commerce and culture of a larger unit was for many Hungarians or Poles axiomatically excluded, just as it seems to be for many Serbs or Romanians today.

Finally, what of the outer frontiers themselves, those porous regions where Europe and Asia meet? Can they be determined with any consistency? The Balkan peninsula, just because it *is* a peninsula, is manifestly part of Europe even at its least European—of what else, after all, could it *be* a part? For its inhabitants there is even something hyper-typically "European" about its past: much of its early modern and modern history is told as the story of struggles against a Turkish imperium, so that Orthodox Christianity, Slavdom, and "Europe" are amalgamated in a real or imagined memory of the fight for liberation from "Asiatic" rule. This gives Greeks, Bulgars, and Serbs their common sense of embattlement—squeezed between central European Catholicism and its Slav allies to their north and the ancient Muslim threat to their south and in their midst.

It also accounts for the urgent Francophilia of many Romanian and Serb intellectuals, who equal and even outdo nineteenth- and twentieth-century Polish writers in their efforts to identify with European culture across the great gulf of uninterest and misunderstanding that separates east and west. Bucharest, today, may seem in many ways only remotely and partly European, but for that very reason, and because of the even more obviously un-European qualities of the remote Romanian countryside, some of its intelligentsia, like that of Belgrade, have always striven to associate with the west, especially France, as an act of defiance against the alien nature of their home environment. The result has all too often been to provoke hyper-nationalism among other local intellectuals and to further alienate the cosmopolitan elite from the popular masses. This, too, is a characteristically "European" pattern.

In the Russian borderlands and in Russia itself, the matter seems less clear. Western observers have always felt ambivalent about Russia's Europeanness, as have many Russians themselves. In language, in religion, in the nature of the state and the imperatives driving it, in its history of contacts and conflicts with other European powers, Russia is recognizably European. But its very size, the fact that most of its borders are with Asiatic peoples to its east and south, and above all the threat it represents for its neighbors to the west all make it seem at least partly alien, not least, of course, in the eyes of those vulnerable neighbors; Communism added nothing and altered little in this respect. For anyone seeking to define Europe, Russia does, though, have two distinct virtues: it marks off the European continent from the lands still farther east: Russia just *is* Europe's eastern boundary. It is also sufficiently distinct from its own western borderlands—which is what the term

"Ukraine" means—to suggest that indeed there is a European Far East, as different from, say, the towns of the Hungarian plain as the latter are from Strasbourg or Turin.

There are thus many "Europes," all with some legitimate claim to the title, none with a monopoly. However, the countries west of the Elbe and Leitha rivers have for a long time *been* Europe, whereas the lands to their east are always somehow in the implied process of *becoming*. We might say, with Voltaire, that there are two Europes: one that "knows" and the other that wants to "become known." In Czeslaw Milosz's understandably different perspective, it is the difference within a family between respectable, upstanding members and a set of embarrassing, slightly annoying, always importuning poor relations. But whatever distinguishes eastern from western Europe certainly did not begin in 1945, or even in 1918; those eighteenth-century travelers and observers who "imagined" Europe's oriental half into existence may have been imposing upon it a prejudiced interpretation deriving from their own concerns, but they did not invent the place from whole cloth.[5]

Nonetheless, relations between eastern and western Europe since the Second World War have taken a novel turn. Thanks to Adolf Hitler, the postwar history of the

5. For an implicitly contrary view, see Wolff, *Inventing Eastern Europe*.

"other" Europe actually resembles that of the western half more than it has ever done before, but through a darkened glass. The eastern Europeans experienced war, civil war, and occupation, but with consequences infinitely more serious and lasting than those in the West. Whereas in France the percentage of the prewar population killed between 1939 and 1945 was 1.75, and in the Netherlands 2.2, in Yugoslavia the military and civilian dead represented 10.6 percent of the prewar population, and in the area of the "General Government" of occupied Poland, 17.9 percent. The Germans targeted eastern Europe's intelligentsia in particular: in the Czech lands, for example, workers, artisans, and peasants did not do at all badly out of the Nazi war economy, but the educated classes were brutalized, imprisoned, and killed in large numbers; in Poland one-third of the interwar graduates from secondary and higher education was exterminated (with the result that in post-1945 Poland perhaps one-fifth of the population was functionally illiterate. As late as the mid-1960s, just 21 percent of state employees had post-primary education—resulting in a grotesquely underqualified and incompetent governing class).

Moreover, the impact of the Nazi occupation, which in France or Belgium helped to encourage the resistance coalitions to think of a fresh postwar start, took the form in occupied eastern Europe of a thoroughgoing social revolution. Here there had frequently been not one occupation but many—in the Yugoslav case, German, Italian, Hungarian, Bulgarian, and Russian. Not only did the Germans sweep away the old elites—notably the educated and professional classes, heavily Jewish in many places[6]—but they were themselves swept away in the afterwash of their defeat. The German communities of the Sudetenland, of Silesia and East Prussia, whole townships of traditionally German language and culture throughout the region, were destroyed or expelled by the postwar governments of Soviet-dominated Europe. The result was a radically altered social landscape: ethnically more homogeneous, socially less variegated, culturally more provincial. Whereas the First World War had brought about frontier changes within which populations mostly stayed in place, after the Second World War frontiers remained mostly unaltered—it was populations that moved, or simply disappeared.[7]

Hitler's social revolution paved the way for Stalin's—indeed, the two are best understood as a single process.

6. However, in eastern Europe as in France, administrative measures against Jews were not always or initially the work of the occupying Germans. It was in February 1939, under the government of the truncated, post-Munich Czech Republic, that Jews were first eliminated from administration, banking, and cultural institutions in the still independent remnant of interwar Czechoslovakia.

7. The exception, as so often, was Poland, which lost 69,000 square miles in its east and gained 40,000 square miles on the west. Here, too, the death of the Jews and the loss of German, Ukrainian, Lithuanian, and Belorussian minorities were most striking: before 1939 Poland had been fully one-third composed of ethnic and religious minorities; in 1947 Poland was 97 percent "Polish."

German takeovers and control of industries and businesses, notably in Czechoslovakia, where the valuable arms industry and its associated manufactures became part of the Nazi war economy, facilitated postwar nationalizations throughout eastern Europe, providing the postwar Communist or coalition governments with arguments from economic convenience in support of their ideological drive toward a state-owned economy.[8] Upward mobility for the children of peasants and workers may have been the goal of the Communist governments, but it was made possible, and even necessary, because the Nazis had gone a long way to destroying the middle classes. By wrecking the (in any case fragile) basis of the rule of law and rights in eastern Europe, the Nazis made it easier for postwar governments there to undermine whatever remained.[9] In their common suspicion of local

8. In 1946, 82 percent of the Yugoslav work force was employed in nationalized industry; by 1948, the comparable figures were 83 percent in Hungary, 84 percent in Poland, 98 percent in Bulgaria. But state ownership of industry was already widespread in Hungary and Poland before the war—partly as a defense against German economic penetration. This argument for retaining the state sector is being heard again today in those same countries.

9. The local memory of crimes committed during the war against neighbors and other civilians (usually Jews), not all of them under German compulsion or instruction, weighed more heavily on postwar eastern Europe than in the west—though not perhaps quite as heavily as one might wish. In any case, here was a further incentive to treat 1945 as a radical departure, putting the past out of mind.

elites, the advantages they offered primary industries at the expense of trade, commerce, and consumption, and their radical reduction of all forms of local autonomy and intermediate institutions, the Germans and Russians, in their consecutive occupations of the lands that separated them, had much more in common than merely their techniques of repression.

Just as the wartime experience of eastern Europe represented a tragically magnified version of that in the West, so its postwar recovery resembled a grotesque parody of that of the western lands. Like western Europe, postwar eastern Europe began with major economic difficulties, inherited political dilemmas, and a multitude of good intentions; young people especially had little attachment to the prewar regimes and were initially enthusiastic for a new start under Communist direction. There was economic planning (begun in most cases well before the Communists secured a monopoly of power), the institution of welfare and social security, reform of landholding, and a general recognition of the need to modernize and rebuild economic plant, already backward and insufficient before 1939 (with the partial exception of Bohemia) and now distorted and badly damaged by six years of war. This much was recognizably "European," and had Marshall Plan aid (rejected under Soviet pressure) and other Western resources and policies been addressed to the difficulties of some of these countries, their prospects, if not radiant, might have been at least interesting.

As it was, of course, the "Europeanizing" of eastern Europe took a very different form. There *was* aid from the West, first in the form of emergency relief at the end of the war, then as loans: between 1945 and 1947 the West (mostly the United States) lent Poland $251 million, Hungary $37 million. But loans to even the smallest west European states were far larger (in the same years Belgium received $310 million, Denmark $272 million, and Greece $161 million) and anyway it all came to a stop, on Stalin's instructions, in 1947. As a result, investment in eastern Europe was almost exclusively local. As in western Europe, the governments in Prague and Warsaw put their efforts into primary resources—coal, heavy industry, transportation infrastructure. But starting from a poorer base, lacking outside assistance, and compelled in any case to follow the Soviet developmental model, they industrialized at the expense of their citizens—squaring the circle of ensuing shortages and discontent by the use of force and terror. In some cases—e.g., in Bohemia—this emphasis upon primitive industrial accumulation actually entailed putting a modern economy into reverse, destroying secondary and consumer-oriented industries in favor of more mines, more steelworks, more chemical factories.

While the crude results were initially impressive—the output of some basic commodities and the growth rate of the primary sector in parts of eastern Europe actually kept pace for a while with western Europe—the long-term effect was disastrous. Not only did eastern

Europe miss the postwar boom, it saddled itself with industrial plant and production strategies that were at once unnecessary, unhealthy, and unpopular. This may have been unclear to some western observers—misled by productivity data and by their own fond wishes— but it was obvious enough to local residents. And the limitations on these impoverished states were in no way overcome by the formal international arrangements set up by the U.S.S.R., pale dysfunctional echoes of their western homologues. COMECON, established in 1949, not only assigned arbitrary production tasks to different nations, thus constraining them to make things that no one wanted and then to buy them from one another at prices fixed in non-negotiable currencies, but also cut its members off from possible markets in the expanding trade arena of western Europe, and this at a moment when parts of eastern Europe might well have stood to benefit from western prosperity—notably from the take-off in West German trading activity during the 1950s. By 1979 the international trade of COMECON members stood at just 9 percent that of world trade as a whole.

Thus eastern Europe's postwar decades differed from those of the West not through a lack of international structures and "unity"—the Warsaw Pact (1955) and COMECON corresponded in form at least to NATO and the EEC—or through an absence of planning and economic coordination but because of the deliberately distorted and self-defeating forms imposed. The association of COMECON with meaningless prices, unwanted goods, and enforced and inappropriate specialization meant that producers and economic planners in eastern Europe, far from thinking in terms of a regional economy or a harmonization of trade and production across national boundaries, became and have remained *especially* suspicious of regional economic agreements or cooperation. For them, thinking "European" means looking to the West. Cooperation with an equally poor neighbor on the east or south not only is of no material benefit but carries with it undesirable memories of a "fraternal" era in which the shared experience of (eastern) "Europe" was repression, inefficiency, poverty, and frustration.

For this reason, and because of their mutually antagonistic paths to national independence, eastern Europeans know remarkably little about one another, for a group of peoples who have for so long lived in close and uncomfortable proximity. The links that matter to them, and the connections they seek, are with civilizations and powers to their west. It is not just their economies that have been non-complementary; cultural links, too, have been rare and disfavored, despite official proclamations to the contrary over the past two generations. Much of the recent history of eastern Europe consists of one people or group of peoples trying to gain land or political or economic advantage at the expense of a neighboring state. The result is a dangerous combination of proximity, ignorance, and mutual scorn.

In a series of polls taken just after the fall of Communism, eastern Europeans were asked to indicate which countries and peoples inspired in them the most (or the least) confidence. For Poles, the Ukrainians came off worst, inspiring no confidence in 75 percent of those questioned; next came the Germans (in whom 70 percent of Poles had no confidence), the Russians (69 percent), and then a sequence of small neighbors—Romanians (64 percent), Belorussians (63 percent), Czechs (61 percent), and so on. For the Czechs, it was Poles and Romanians who came off worst (77 percent each), followed by Hungarians (67 percent) and Bulgarians (62 percent). Russians (62 percent) and Germans especially (44 percent) were better regarded, which says something about the differences between Polish and Czech memories of the war. But *all* these percentages are notably higher than comparable polls taken among western Europeans.[10]

What is suggested here is that Communism not only froze certain sorts of domestic prejudice in the lands over which it held sway, discouraging public expression of

10. In polls taken among western Europeans today, a generally positive feeling is expressed about most other members of the European Union. The striking exception is that neither Italians nor Greeks have much confidence in their own fellow nationals! Where just 11 percent of the British and Dutch, in a 1981 poll, showed mistrust of their fellow citizens, the figures were more than three times as high among Italians. To be fair, no one had any confidence in the Greeks.

anti-Jewish or anti-Gypsy sentiment, for example, yet doing nothing to dispel it, but actually encouraged and exacerbated many interstate resentments that had been formed in the struggles for national independence during the later nineteenth century and in the interwar years when new states enjoyed a brief moment of fragile independence. After 1918 as before, the only institutional options for the peoples of eastern Europe were either one-nation states along the western model, or else being part of multinational units of the old, imperial kind. As it was, a whole series of independent micro-multinational units arose, nation-states with multiple ethnic minorities, the worst of both worlds.[11]

The hatreds generated within and among these new units—between Serbs and Croats, Serbs and Hungarians, Romanians and Hungarians, Hungarians and Slovaks, Slovaks and Czechs, Czechs and Germans, Germans and Poles, Poles and Czechs, and many others besides —were first exploited and then forcibly repressed by Hitler and by Stalin. The obligatory "fraternity" of the Communist years, and the virtual impossibility of estab-

11. A 1946 census revealed the following breakdown of the population of Yugoslavia, for example: 6.5 million Serbs, 3.8 million Croats, 1.4 million Slovenes, 800,000 Muslim Bosnians, 800,000 Macedonians, 750,000 Albanians, 496,000 Hungarians, and 400,000 Montenegrins, as well as Vlachs, Gypsies, Bulgarians, Jews, Germans, Turks, Romanians, and Greeks.

lishing economic and political relations with any but neighboring socialist states, did the rest. Although there are some (notably in Budapest and Vienna) who would gratefully return to the old Austro-Hungarian Empire, the fact is that throughout eastern and central Europe international solutions to local problems are at a discount (the hyper-Jacobin quality of Communist rule in eastern Europe shares the responsibility for this post-1989 political centrifugalism).

Understandably, then, the very idea of "Europe" has taken on a rather different and special meaning in the countries once ruled from Moscow. As in western Europe, a certain image conjured up by the very word was called forth against the miseries and mistakes of the past. But this did not happen before the 1970s; until then the attention of domestic opponents of Stalinist regimes was still directed toward the prospects for a "reformed" or "revised" Communism. Only after 1968 (and in Poland the strikes and repression of 1970) did a new generation of dissident intellectuals like Adam Michnik and Václav Havel arise, for whom Marxism was the problem, not the solution, and for whom "Europe" represented an alternative to the present as much as to the past. For these internal critics of the failed Communist regimes, the solution was increasingly a "return to Europe."

This is a curious and protean expression; at once geographical—"we" wish to be part of the European family, and not just the western edge of the Soviet one;

nostalgic—"we" who were once the heart of European music, literature, philosophy, and the arts aspire to rejoin the community we helped to shape; political—"our" traditions in law, in political institutions, in human freedoms are European, and we want them back; and economic—"Europe" today signifies a community of flourishing free economies and we want to be in it and of it. But there are difficulties with this way of criticizing Communist regimes and seeking to emerge from under them. In the first place, it implicitly acknowledges that "eastern" Europe is somehow not quite Europe and is trying to find its way in (or, more controversially, back). Heinrich Heine famously noted that baptism was, for Jews, their "European entry ticket." Similarly, for citizens of Poland, Hungary, Slovenia, et al., membership in the Union is *their* entry ticket. But, as Heine well knew, baptism was no solution. An assimilated, even a converted, Jew remained a Jew, Europeanized or no. And as every eastern European knows, the mere fact of being accorded membership in a Western club would not wipe away the effects of fifty-plus years of terror, dictatorship, repression, and stagnation.

Secondly, "thinking European" in formerly Communist eastern Europe carries very distinctive implications. To the extent that Communism stood for an artificial and enforced internationalization, an equally effective way of opposing it was to emphasize—or reemphasize—the standing and distinction of the locality, the nation, to exalt Polish, or Hungarian, or Czech particularity over Soviet universalism. And if "international" Communism was vulnerable to the criticisms of nationalists, so is "Europe." Thus despite being utterly different, even opposites, in the imagination of some of the best-known dissidents, "Europeanness," the elective affinity—the moral capital—of the opponents of Communism, can readily be equated by intellectuals and politicians of a nationalist bent with the now discredited transnational universalism of Communism. That is why the smartest Communist apparatchiks, in Belgrade, Bucharest, Kiev, Zagreb, and Bratislava, have been quick to recycle themselves into nationalist demagogues.[12]

In western Europe, by contrast, except in the most extreme nationalist circles of France, Austria, and among subsections of the British political class, there is nothing especially controversial today about being "European"— it carries no suggestion of the lack of properly "national" sentiment. To be "European" does not entail casting aspersions upon your fellow citizens, nor does it imply keeping one's distance from them. This is a real and significant achievement for the European Union, and one worth emphasizing.

12. Professor Kathleen Verdery quotes an editorial in one Romanian nationalist paper: "To us [the National Party] the temptation of the Common European Home is a utopia every bit as damaging as communism." From an unpublished paper, "Civil Society or Nation? 'Europe' in Romania's post-Socialist politics."

It would be too easy to dismiss the importance of nationalist sentiment in eastern Europe. It is, after all, a part of the world where nations and states have a habit of disappearing, their institutions, religions, languages, and people suppressed or expelled by empires or competitors.[13] But it is not accorded to everyone to have the good fortune to be at once nationally secure and effortlessly universal—that is why so many eastern European intellectuals long for and envy Paris, the place and the image alike. In the meantime, at home, they and their pro-European electoral allies risk political marginalization by seeming to pay more attention to an abstraction (and an uncaring and unresponsive one at that) than to the immediate needs of their fellow citizens. The renascence of anti-Semitism in parts of eastern Europe (or rather its relegitimization in party politics—it never really died) is closely related to the negative connotations of cosmopolitanism and elitism. In short, "Europe-ism" is now attached to the pre-1989 opposition in Hungary,

13. To cosmopolitan observers the local obsession with such territory and traditions as these countries have managed to acquire and retain can seem petty and provincial; at once grandiose and absurd. Thus Heine, again, writing in 1823: "Observing how effectively a national literature contributes to national preservation (this may sound ridiculous but is nevertheless true, and was told me in all seriousness by many Poles), they are attempting to create a national literature in Warsaw."

Poland, and elsewhere (many of whose most prominent activists were, indeed, Jewish).[14]

Since 1989 the term "Europe" has acquired further, unflattering associations in the formerly Communist states. Not only does the word conjure up images of cosmopolitan, rootless intellectuals with their hearts in Paris and their pockets in New York, it also denotes the wealthy, privileged, harsh laissez-faire world that the West now seeks to impose with no thought for the resulting social disruption and economic insecurity. Worse, the leaders of that same "Europe" don't even want to allow those on whom they would impose its draconian requirements to join the club once they have accepted the rules! No wonder, as the Polish premier Hanna Suchocka noted in 1992, a "growing anti-European" sentiment could be felt in Poland.

Subsequent elections there and elsewhere have confirmed her fears. Rooted in distaste for the new but no less wooden language of post-Communism ("market," "inflation," "redundancy," "growth rates" are cold terms of art insensitive to the requirements and sufferings of real people), this suspicion of Europe, in Poland as else-

14. In a poll published in *Gazeta Wyborcza* in August 1992, 40 percent of Poles questioned believed that "people of Jewish nationality [*sic*] play too large a role in the public life of the country." Recent pronouncements (in June 1995) by a Catholic priest in Gdansk, from which then President Walesa declined to disassociate himself, suggest that such sentiments are not confined to the street.

where, has converted readily into votes for the recycled ex-Communist politicians who play off it so skillfully. For the inefficiency and usually illusory nature of full employment, social services, and other familiar "comforts" eastern Europe enjoyed under Communism should not blind us to the fears and resentment aroused by their loss. Just as anything "capitalist" was the object of uncritical admiration by nearly everyone living under Communism—because of the unremitting and unselective criticism to which capitalism was subjected by the Soviet regime—so "Communism," comprehensively dismissed by its democratic heirs, may yet acquire some of the same aura for those who have suffered in the transition since 1989.

Under these circumstances, it is not easy to be a "European" in eastern Europe. Typically, one is the object of multiple exclusions: populists charge you with a lack of local and national feeling; you may be resented for having opposed the old Communist regimes at a time when most people were making greater or lesser compromises—in short, you are an unwelcome reminder of the recent past and thus an uncomfortable source of embarrassment. Meanwhile for western Europeans with whom you would otherwise identify, you remain at best an admirable "exception," at worst an exotic curio. It is, after all, with the so-called realistic post-'89 politicians that the West does its business—most of whom (like the Czech Republic's Václav Klaus) took little or no part in the pre-1989 opposition. These new, practical "Euròpeans" of eastern Europe negotiate as best they can for admission to the club. But in their hands the Europe envisaged and idealized by Adam Michnik in Poland or János Kis in Hungary, student radicals of the sixties who became courageous public dissidents in the following decades, is all but invisible. The Europe of culture, of freedoms, of the cosmopolitan circulation of knowledge and values, the Europe that Milan Kundera feared was losing its heart as Czechoslovakia and others drifted into the Russian orbit—*this* Europe has few advocates in the East today.

One explanation for this is the growing awareness among eastern Europeans, intellectuals and politicians alike, of how little they matter for the West. This is not a new theme, of course. Part of what it means to be an eastern European is to be perennially disappointed by the West—from the Polish revolutionaries of 1830 to Munich, from the insurrectionary Czechs of 1945, for-lornly awaiting Patton's tanks, to Czeslaw Milosz in 1951 or Milan Kundera in 1984 trying to explain to western readers why the "East" matters and how much it hangs on their response, from the pathos of Hungarian radio messages in November 1956 to the tragedy of Bos-nian appeals for help in 1995. There is a depressing innocence about the number of times eastern Europeans have sought to explain to western audiences why it is in the latter's own interest to take into account the needs and desires of their admirers and allies in the middle of

Europe—and over and over again the answer has been that they just don't count, in the larger scheme of things.[15] In some ways the most surprising thing about the Yalta arrangements—or the November 1944 "percentages agreement" between Stalin and Churchill, by which the two statesmen ended a convivial evening by jotting down the "share" of postwar influence that the Western Allies and the Soviet Union would have in eastern and central Europe—was that any attention was paid to eastern Europe at all.

The lands separating Russia from Germany have understandably mattered a lot more to those two states, just as the Balkans did to Austria and Turkey. The historic shadow of Russia, for whom eastern Europe rep-

---

15. For British views, see the conclusions of a Cabinet subcommittee in 1944, which listed four areas of vital interest to be considered when dealing with the Soviet Union; none of them concerned eastern Europe. They were Middle Eastern oil; the Mediterranean; "vital sea communications"; industrial relations and production in Britain. See Hugh Thomas, *Armed Truce: The Beginnings of the Cold War 1945–1946* (New York, 1987), p. 209.

As for France, it was Charles de Gaulle who in May 1968, during a visit to Romania, told Nicolae Ceauçescu that "a regime like yours is useful here and in the Soviet Union—but would be impossible in France or Great Britain." This was almost certainly a sincere expression of de Gaulle's belief that eastern Europe was a different world from that of the West, where different political values could be applied. See Sandra Stolojan, *Avec de Gaulle en Roumanie* (Paris, 1991).

resented a western imperial frontier, vulnerable and imprecise, is a matter of simple political geography; the German presence in the modern era has been much more a question of economics. Germany's role in the area was already marked before the First World War, but became overwhelming thereafter: in the last year before the outbreak of the Second World War, 58 percent of Bulgaria's imports came from Germany and 64 percent of its exports went there; for Yugoslavia the figures were 50 percent and 49 percent, for Romania 49 percent and 36 percent. As now, this unequal para-colonial relationship with Germany is the only truly "European" heritage that most eastern Europeans have been able to claim. For the western powers their countries were of historical or at most tactical interest, lacking resources and sitting athwart no vital lines of communication.

Western intellectual taste since the Enlightenment has also tended to favor large, universal propositions and prospects. From the Jacobins to the Communists, therefore, western leftists (who might otherwise have been expected to take a greater interest in the social and ethnic problems of the region) have shown more sympathy for large territorial units and standardized social practices. The besetting sin of eastern Europe has been its very particularism, which is why Russian, German, and British thinkers have often thought that European affairs would be better managed if the continent's central and eastern areas could just be attached to one or more historic states (or subdivided among them—the late-eighteenth-century Polish partitions, when the country was cynically carved up among Russia, Prussia, and Austria in the years 1772–95, are a good metaphor for the subsequent history of the region as a whole).[16]

To be sure, parts of east-central Europe have been sufficiently "preserved," albeit against their will, to represent a sort of museum of Europe's recent past—western visitors to post-Communist eastern Europe were sometimes smitten with a sort of secondhand nostalgia for an earlier, slower, dirtier, safer, older western Europe, now swept away beyond recall by the depredations of prosperity. And for many readers in the United States and Germany especially, the writings of Václav Havel, with their high moral tone and neo-Heideggerian distaste for the trappings and soullessness of "modernity," were unusual and refreshing enough to have seemed appealing, for a passing moment. But in the end the in-

16. For the latest instance of such a dismissive approach see Eric J. Hobsbawm, *The Age of Extremes* (New York, 1994), where the author does little to hide his irritation at the downfall of the Soviet empire and the consequent revival of the small countries on its western fringes. For an earlier example of the same cast of mind, see G.D.H. Cole, *Europe, Russia and the Future*. Writing in 1941, Cole, a British historian of left-leaning sympathies, thought that indefensible sovereign states in eastern Europe had no future and that it would be better if a victorious postwar Soviet Union simply absorbed Poland, Hungary, and the Balkans.

tellectuals of eastern (or, as they would have it, central) Europe can have few illusions. Having stood for a Europe in which there would be no east–west division and where the preserved (or remembered) culture of central Europe would take its rightful place once more, they must now realize that the very price of their liberation is renewed marginality, at home and abroad.

For eastern Europe, in any event, there is but one option; joining western Europe on the latter's terms. Put thus, it is a choice likely to generate angry and resentful opposition from nationalists of all sorts. But the only historical alternative is, once again, to look east—there is no secure middle ground. Except for some Serbs, even the most national-populist of east European politicians can find little solace in the prospect of alliance with, friendship with, or even informal affiliation to a renascent Russia. After Versailles the small states of eastern Europe took France as their model and protector; after 1932 they turned, more or less reluctantly, to Germany; from 1944 to 1989 the U.S.S.R. was their only realistic option. Now it is "Europe."

And so "Europe" it is, on "Europe's" terms. This is now the last remaining article of common political faith among democrats in eastern Europe: that because they just *are* a part of Europe the lands of liberated eastern Europe will indeed become a place in it. For political leaders it is a desperate medium-term gamble: if they can get accepted into prosperous, secure "Europe," then the sacrifices they have asked of their electorate—loss of employment and security, acceptance of inequalities and risks—will have been worth it. If they are rejected, or kept waiting too long, or accepted on meaningless or partial terms, then "Europe" will become an ever more derogatory term in nationalist parlance, and the backlash against the attempt to join the West—and by extension against the revolutions of 1989—could be serious indeed.

For the intellectuals who first put the "return to Europe" on the agenda the situation is equally depressing. They are already back in Europe, their presence sometimes more eagerly sought in Vienna or in Paris than in their own hometowns. But they have failed in their larger project of making their own cultures (Czech, Polish, Hungarian, Croatian) a presence within the culture of Europe as a whole—an enterprise whose forlorn and illusory quality is just what made it so distinctively "central European." The interest in things eastern (more accurately "central") European so enthusiastically aroused in the 1980s has largely died down. Like the Americans, western Europeans are concerned more with Russia than with its former satellites, and with their own domestic concerns more than with the foreign aspirations of their eastern neighbors. Would-be "European" peoples of former multinational states, such as Czechs or Slovenes, have been made to feel less welcome than they had expected. But the hope remains that even if western Europe will never fully recognize and appreciate on equal terms the distinctive qualities of the other Europeans, it will at least be true to its own principles and accord them the right to join the rest of the continent. If we cannot be of Europe, the latter might say, we shall at least be in it. Is this, too, an illusion?

## 3

# GOODBYE TO ALL THAT?

"IN THE first years after the war . . . Europeans took shelter behind a collective amnesia" (Hans-Magnus Enzensberger). This drive to forget and build anew was remarkably successful. The Cold War began just two years after the defeat of Hitler; the Korean War three years later; shortly after it ended, the West European economic miracle began. There was no time, and certainly no incentive, to come to terms with the real experience of war and occupation—no time, as it were, to mourn. The revolutionary civil wars that had been threatening to break out all over the continent in 1945 were snuffed out and their origins buried in a heap of collective self-congratulation: "we" won the war, "we" resisted, "we" are going to build a new and better Europe.

Had it not been for the rapidity with which western Europeans especially put the war behind them, the reconstruction of many postwar European states, not to mention any European community, would have been much more difficult. But the result was that "Europe" has been peculiarly vulnerable to a return of memory—the past is a burden on the present, as well as a source of understanding. Ernest Renan was right to conclude that "L'oubli et je dirais même l'erreur historique, sont un facteur essentiel de l'histoire d'une nation et c'est ainsi que le progrès des études historiques est souvent pour la nationalité un danger."[1]

But it was not historical studies that undermined the easy certainties of the postwar settlement. It was history itself. Of course, historical studies played their part; the investigation of Vichy France (notably and symptomatically the research published by a foreign scholar, Robert Paxton of Columbia University); the *Historikerstreit* in West Germany, a public debate among historians and others over the uniqueness or otherwise of the Nazi experience in general and the extermination of Jews in particular; the renewal of Austrian historiography in the aftermath of the revelations about Kurt Waldheim and his "mismemory" of wartime military service; the first tentative questionings in Italy of the myth of anti-Fascism, notably in the work of Claudio Pavone on the Italian civil war of 1943–45—these have all contributed to a more complex picture of the Europe of 1945 and

1. "Forgetting, and I would even say historical error, are essential elements in the history of a nation, and the progress of historical scholarship is thus often a threat to national identity." From *What Is a Nation?*

its burdensome inheritance.[2] But what truly altered the picture, and may be said to have brought the postwar era to a belated end, was the developments of 1989.

For the end of Communism was also the beginning of memory. The truth of this proposition in the formerly Communist lands themselves is self-evident. What could not be said, or even known, about the history and politics of central and eastern Europe for sixty years has now risen to the surface, and it has often provoked strenuous efforts at renewed repression of different but no less uncomfortable memories.[3] In former East Germany an optimistic belief that economic prosperity would bring the divided country together and wash away unhappy memories—an attempt, in short, to reproduce the "economic miracle" of the Federal Republic and its attendant benefits—has foundered not so much on the presence of those memories but upon the absence of any

2. The multiple layers of self-induced amnesia in Austria in particular are impressive indeed. In addition to preferring to glide over the repressions of 1934, the enthusiasms of 1938, and the criminal participation that followed, Austrians and Austrian historiography have yet to come fully to terms with the deeply undeserved ease with which their country reentered the postwar "European family," not to mention the benefits that accrued to the country from four decades of smug neutralism.
3. I have discussed this theme more fully in "The Past Is Another Country: Myth and Memory in Postwar Europe," *Daedalus* (121:iv), Fall 1992.

economic transformation comparable to that which West Germany enjoyed in the early 1950s.

Yet in the West the morally disruptive effect of 1989 has been paradoxically greater than in the East. Most eastern Europeans knew, after all, that they were living a lie, that the official accounts of their past and their present bore little relation to remembered experience or contemporary observation. The "trauma" of 1989 for most people in the once Communist states consists primarily of socioeconomic disruption and political disappointment. But for westerners multiple layers of illusion and silence wait to be addressed. The dilemma is most acute in France. Just as they began to emerge, chastened, from what Henry Rousso dubbed the Vichy syndrome, from sobering encounters with their wartime past and four decades of inability to acknowledge it, the French are now facing a serious challenge to everything they have been taught to believe about their place in postwar Europe.

The essence of the Franco-German condominium around which Western Europe was built lay in a mutually convenient arrangement: that the Germans would have the economic means and the French would retain the political initiative. In the very first years, of course, the Germans had not yet acquired their present wealth and French predominance was real. But from the mid-1950s this was no longer true; thereafter France's hegemony in West European affairs rested upon a nuclear weapon that the country could not use, an army that it could not deploy within the continent itself, and an international political standing derived largely from the self-interested magnanimity of the three victorious Powers at the end of the war. The unspoken premise of France's relations with West Germany was this: you pretend not to be powerful and we'll pretend not to notice that you are.

Franco-German relations in the 1960s and '70s resembled nothing so much as those of Austria and Prussia in the early nineteenth century. The Austrians saw no great danger, and some advantage, in Prussia's becoming rich and influential among the industrializing north Germans, so long as the Habsburgs were recognized as the senior partner in German-speaking Europe and respected accordingly. By the time they realized that formal seniority was an empty honor and that Prussian prosperity carried with it both the desire for extended influence and the capacity to enforce that desire, it was too late: defeated and then patronized, the Austrians were a secondary power with no role inside a henceforth united Germany. Of course, there is no question of France suffering yet another (military) defeat at German hands, but in all other respects the analogy is revealing.

Thus 1989, with the collapse of the Iron Curtain and the creation of a Germany far larger and wealthier than France, brought to an end a unique period in French diplomatic history. From 1951 to 1989 France has enjoyed that special freedom of action—and an accompanying illusion of real power—that comes from being

TONY JUDT

allied to a strong but unthreatening neighbor and being, for the first time in centuries, well distanced from the only possible threat to its security, far to the east. What this easy political primacy hid from most French eyes was the steady decline in France's real presence in Europe.

One economic datum may illustrate the point. In 1990 a chart of French economic influence (measured by the reciprocal importance of its trade with other countries) would show that the presence of France was limited to the states in the Europe of Nine—that is to say, the original Six plus Britain, Ireland, and Denmark. Germany, in contrast, already encompassed within its range of economic influence not only the Europe of Fifteen but also most of the rest of the continent to the south and east. The significance of this is clear. Between 1951 and 1990 France did little more than stand its ground while the German economy expanded across the whole continent. France had become a regional power, confined to Europe's western edge; Germany, even before unification, was once again the great power of Europe.

The shock of this has been all the greater in that it had suited everyone to deny it as long as possible. Precisely because they did emerge from the Second World War so humiliated (a humiliation further worsened by military defeat in Vietnam, civil conflict in North Africa, and the collapse of the Fourth Republic in 1958), the French had every reason to insist on playing a dominant role in a little Europe—where, as we have seen, their interests were especially represented. But in some ways the impact of 1989 has been equally problematic for the Germans. For just as weakness and declining international power arouse difficult memories for France, so in Germany does an apparent excess of power. German politicians from Adenauer to Helmut Kohl had made a point of playing down German strength, deferring to French political initiatives, and emphasizing their own wish for nothing more than a stable Germany in a prosperous Europe; they have thus fallen victim to their own rhetoric, bequeathing to post-1989 Europe a muscle-bound state with no sense of national purpose.

As a consequence, Germany's national agenda today is a little too full. In addition to the economic and political problem of absorbing the eastern *Länder*, Germans must come to terms with the paradox of *Ostpolitik*: that many German politicians, especially on the left, were well pleased with things the way they were and would have been quite content to see the Wall remain a little longer. Before 1989 West Germans, especially Social Democrats, did not want to hear about political persecution in the GDR; *Ostpolitik* and *détente* had priority. More than one former East German dissident recalls this, though most West Germans have consigned it to a memory-hole. Germans also have to reckon with embarrassments about their own capacities—now that they can and manifestly do lead Europe, where should they take it? And of what Europe are they the natural leaders: the west-leaning "Europe" forged by the French, or that traditional Europe of German interests, where Germany sits not on the eastern edge but squarely in the middle? Here, too, memories flood in. A Germany at the heart of Europe carries echoes and reminders that many people, Germans perhaps most of all, have sought since 1949 to set aside. But the image of a Germany attached fervently but not very logically to its western frontiers as though these alone stood between the nation and its demons is not very convincing.

Amid the endless barrage of Euro-debates—about a single currency, monetary union, open (or closed) frontiers, standardization, and majority voting, all of them topics that have been on the Euro-table in some form or another since 1955 or before—only one issue matters: is Europe to be extended? If so, how far and on what terms? The further the extension and the more binding the terms, the more Germany's centrality must become obvious. France, which has spent forty comfortable years in a restricted, peripheral Europe, has every reason to fear such an extension: not because it actually represents any shift in the balance of power on the continent, but because it confirms that the shift has been steadily taking place. The alternative, given that Europe cannot by its own account stay still, is to devote more time to perfecting—and preserving—the institutions of "real existing Europe" and to postpone its eastward extension (except on meaningless terms) as long as possible.

But what if both Germany and France were laboring under a continued illusion (their politicians, at least—

opinion polls suggest that voters in both countries are increasingly skeptical of Euro-promises)—and encouraging others to do likewise? What if the real problem with post-1989 Europe is the one that the late President Mitterrand implicitly feared and sought to avert: that any attempt to take it further can be achieved only at the cost of its gains to date? That a united Europe, in short, has become a zero-sum game in which the extension of its benefits to newcomers from the east will be achieved only at some real cost to the current members? This is not a new idea, of course; similar fears and calculations lay behind the doubts expressed by some when first Greece, then Spain and Portugal were taken on board. But it may be a fear whose time has come.

Can the European Union in its present form absorb the countries of former Communist Europe? In economic terms alone, it would make for onerous and unpopular burdens. In the 1992 EC budget, only four countries were net contributors: Germany, Great Britain, France, and the Netherlands (in descending order of per capita contribution); the beneficiaries, in the same order per capita, were Luxembourg, Ireland, Greece, Belgium, Portugal, Denmark, Spain, and Italy. True, the subsequent newcomers—Sweden, Finland, and Austria—are all potential contributors, but their economies are small and their share will not amount to much. Conversely, *all* conceivable future members of the Union (Switzerland apart) fall unambiguously into the category of beneficiaries.

It has been estimated (in a 1994 study by the Bertelsmann Foundation) that the four "Visegrad Group" countries—Poland, the Czech Republic, Slovakia, and Hungary—alone would cost the European Union DM 20 billion per annum in direct payments: more than is currently given to Spain, Portugal, Greece, and Ireland combined. Romania, Bulgaria, and others would cost more still—and would contribute even less. The standard of living of the most advanced of the "candidate countries"—Hungary and the Czech Republic—is less than half that of the average for the present European Union, and for the poorer ones it is more like one-fifth the average. In Jane Kramer's words, "The idea of 'Europe' had been moving only as long as no-one suffered from it, or thought he suffered." Whether or not anyone would be seen as "suffering," it is clear that it would cost the Union a lot of money—more than it can presently afford—to bring in such future members *on the same terms as present ones.*

And then there are the non-economic considerations. It is not thought very good form to raise the issue in Europe today, but most of the east European countries do not remotely qualify for membership in the Union under certain existing rules, notably those for the protection of rights of individuals and minorities—religious, national, or ethnic. The vulnerability of the Hungarian minorities in Romania and Slovakia and the abusive treatment to which Gypsies are subjected throughout the region exclude many of these states from membership under present rules, as do the de facto limits upon press freedom in Slovakia and Romania, and restrictions upon the news media in most of the region, Poland being a laudable exception. Some of the same criticisms could also be addressed to Greece, with respect to its discrimination against Albanians and other non-Orthodox groups living within its territory, not to mention its unneighborly treatment of the new Macedonian state to its north. But the presence of one semi-democratic Balkan state within "Europe" is no grounds for extending the hypocritical exception to other candidates.

One source of the present, difficult situation is the fact that the European Union is not as prosperous as it used to be. Had the Berlin Wall fallen, say, in 1971, there would have been many of the same misgivings about extending the benefits of EEC membership to liberated Easterners but less real economic difficulty in doing so—the burden would have been approximately comparable to that currently borne by Germany as the price for its own unification. What has changed in between is the rate of economic growth and perceived well-being of the West itself. The great oil crisis of 1974 had a severe impact on even the strongest European economies: in the Federal Republic, GNP actually *fell* by 0.5 percent in 1974 and again, by 1.6 percent, in 1975, unprecedented blips in the postwar *Wirtschaftswunder*. In 1981 and 1982 it declined by 0.2 percent and 1 percent respectively. In Italy the GNP fell (by 3.7

percent) in 1976, for the first time since the end of the war. Neither the German nor any other Western European economy has ever been the same again. This should come as no surprise. In 1950 Western Europe depended upon oil for only 8.5 percent of its energy needs; most of the rest, as we have seen, was provided by coal, Europe's indigenous and cheap fossil fuel. By 1970 oil accounted for 60 percent of European energy consumption. The quadruple increase in oil prices thus put an end to a quarter of a century of cheap energy, sharply and definitively raising the cost of manufacture, transport, and daily living.

The effect of this on the European Community itself was severe. An important feature of the Community had been its capacity to serve with equal success the very different needs of its member countries, needs deriving from interwar experiences and memories that differed quite markedly. The Belgians (like the British) feared unemployment more than anything else; the French wanted above all to avoid the Malthusian stagnation of earlier decades; Germans lived in terror of an unstable, inflated currency. After 1974 the stalled economy of Europe threatened a distinctive nemesis to each and all: increasing unemployment, an end to growth, and sharply rising prices.

There has thus been an unanticipated return to earlier woes. The cycle of endless growth, with stable currencies and near-full employment, was broken in the seventies and never recovered. Far from being able to offer the advantages of an economic miracle to an ever-expanding community of beneficiaries, "Europe" can no longer even be sure of being able to provide them to itself. The events of 1989 placed this problem on the agenda, but the origins of the Union's inability to address it began fifteen years before. And at its heart, precisely because it marks such a break with the promise of earlier decades, lies the problem of unemployment.

The memory of unemployment between the wars varies from country to country. It was never a great scourge in France, averaging just 3.3 percent per annum throughout the 1930s. But in Britain, where 7.5 percent of the labor force was already unemployed during the 1920s, the annual average of 11.5 percent in the thirties was something that politicians and economists of every stripe swore should never happen again. In Belgium and Germany, where the unemployment rate was nearly 9 percent, similar sentiments obtained. It was thus one of the glories of the postwar European economy that it maintained close to full employment through much of the 1950s and 1960s in northern and western Europe. In the 1960s the annual average unemployment rate in Western Europe was just 1.6 percent. In the following decade it rose to an annual average of 4.2 percent. By the late 1980s it had doubled again, with annual average rates of unemployment in the EC at 9.2 percent; by 1993 the figure stood at 11 percent.

Within these already depressing figures lurked patterns that were more truly disturbing. In 1993 unemployment among men and women under twenty-five exceeded 20 percent in six EC countries (Spain, Ireland, France, Italy, Belgium, and Greece). Even more revealingly, the *long-term* unemployed accounted for more than one-third the total of those without work in those six nations as well as the U.K., the Netherlands, and the former West Germany. Even in the prosperous new candidates for membership in December 1993, both Finland and Sweden had high rates of youth unemployment, and the overall national figure for unemployment in Finland was 16 percent. The redistributive impact of the inflation of the 1980s worsens the effect of these figures, widening the gap between people in work and the unemployed. What is more, upturns in the economy no longer have the effect, as they did during the boom years, of absorbing surplus labor and pulling up the worse-off. Who now remembers the fantasies of the 1960s, when it was blithely believed that production problems had been solved, and all that remained was to adjust distribution and avoid excess?

The combination of rapid growth—with cities expanding, and urban and suburban communities being transformed—and subsequent economic stagnation has brought to Western Europe not only a renewed threat of economic insecurity, something unknown to most Europeans since the late 1940s, but also greater social disruption and physical risk than at any time since the early Industrial Revolution. All over Western Europe today one sees desolate satellite towns, rotting suburbs, and hopeless city ghettos. Even the great capital cities —London, Paris, Rome—are neither as clean, as safe, nor as hopeful as they were just thirty years ago. They and dozens of provincial cities from Lyons to Lübeck are developing an urban underclass, divided between those, usually foreign, often dark, who are hated and those (young, predominantly male, almost exclusively white) who do the hating. If these depressing developments of the last twenty years have not had more explosive social and political consequences, the credit lies with the systems of social welfare with which Western Europeans furnished themselves after 1945.

Welfare, in its multiple forms, is *the* great West European achievement of recent years. It is what distinguishes the region not only from the United States, where there is almost no formal community provision for the health and protection of all its members, but also from eastern Europe, where the provisions were formal but often not much more. In addition to its unquestioned social benefits, the welfare state proved particularly effective at serving as a political safety valve—were this not so, the recent economic depression might well have had disastrous effects, comparable to those of the 1840s or 1930s, long since calling into question any lingering illusions about the indefinite survival of postwar stability.

Like so much else in Europe since 1945, the increased provision of welfare and social services drew directly upon the memory of the interwar years, remembered as an experience never to be repeated. It is no coincidence that those nations that had it worst in the 1930s placed themselves at the forefront of social reform afterward. Unemployment in Scandinavia had been higher than anywhere else in prewar Europe (reaching 42 percent of the labor force in Denmark and Norway in 1932–33, 31.5 percent in Sweden). From the start, then, in Scandinavia and in Britain, the postwar welfare state differed from its more hesitant Continental counterpart: there were universal social rights, sharply progressive taxes, diminished income differentials, flat-rate benefits, and central provision of essential services. Between 1945 and 1951 the Labour government in Britain was spending about 10 percent of the national income on various social services and provisions; in Denmark 9.8 percent, in Sweden 8.9 percent, in Norway 7.8 percent. By 1973, when the first serious hints of tax revolt surfaced on the electoral landscape, the Scandinavians were all spending at least 22 percent of their national income in this way.

The rest of Europe followed rather more slowly. The Christian Democratic governments of Italy (led by Alcide De Gasperi), West Germany (directed by Chancellor Adenauer), and France (where Georges Bidault's Mouvement Républicain Populaire was in office for most of the first decade following the liberation) were less enthusiastically in favor of "cradle to grave" social services; but among them, too, there was a broad consensus on the need for a high and sustained level of state spending on education, health, housing, social insurance, and retirement. Given that defense spending was low and falling for most of the period, the overall expenditures of governments, as a percentage of the Gross Domestic Product, are a reasonable indicator of the place of spending on welfare and related areas in the national economy as a whole. Growing slowly between 1938 and 1950, the rate of government expenditures took off dramatically over the next quarter of a century—in economies that were themselves expanding very fast:

### Table 1
(Government Spending as a Percentage
of Gross Domestic Product)

|             | 1938 | 1950 | 1973 |
|-------------|------|------|------|
| France      | 23.2 | 27.6 | 38.8 |
| Germany[4]  | 42.4 | 30.4 | 42.0 |
| Netherlands | 21.7 | 6.8  | 45.5 |
| U.K.        | 28.8 | 34.2 | 41.5 |

The chief beneficiaries of these burgeoning public services were adults who remembered harder times and who saw nothing wrong in paying for improved security through higher taxes or, in the French case, through substantial social security payments by employers. With everyone employed and (thanks to the postwar baby boom) a majority of the population young and ever

4. The high German figure is of course explained by the Nazis' heavy public outlays, not least on weapons and the military.

healthier, the welfare states appeared to be actuarially well founded. But they depended upon flourishing economies to sustain the employment that paid for them. Once unemployment became endemic, the cost of looking after those without work fell proportionately ever harder upon those still employed, at once reducing available resources and placing strains upon the collective solidarity of a community now dividing more obviously into givers and receivers.

More even than unemployment, the chief hazard facing the welfare states of Western Europe is the simple fact that the population is aging. The baby boom peaked in 1964, a little later in Mediterranean Europe. Ever since then the general trend has been for fewer children per family, to the point that in some countries, notably Italy and Spain, the population is not even maintaining itself. In Spain the birth rate per thousand in 1993 was just 1.1, a historic low. In one sense this tendency is not such bad news: as demand for labor falls, it may not matter that there is less labor to be had, though troughs in the birth rate wreak havoc with employment and planning in the educational services. But in the meantime Europeans must support a large and growing population of older people on the backs of fewer and fewer younger people, many of whom are not employed. A system designed for flourishing economies when a large number of employed young people supported the social needs of a relatively small population of the old and sick is now under serious pressure.

In northern and western Europe the population aged sixty-five and over has grown by between 12 percent and 17 percent (depending on the country) since the mid-1960s. Moreover, even those under sixty-five can no longer be counted automatically on the "productive" side of the national equation: in West Germany the percentage of men aged sixty to sixty-four who were in paid employment fell from 72 to 44 in the two decades after 1960; in the Netherlands the figures were 81 and 58 respectively. At the moment the underemployed elderly are merely an expensive burden. But once the baby boomers begin to retire (around 2010 A.D.), the presence of a huge, frustrated, bored, unproductive, and ultimately unhealthy population of old people could become a major social crisis. It should already be a matter of some concern that the far-right populist parties of Jörg Haider in Austria and Jean-Marie Le Pen in France do notably better among unemployed youth and the insecure aged than among employed persons in the prime of life.

It is clear to most European politicians that the costs of maintaining the welfare state in its maximal form cannot be carried indefinitely. The difficulty lies in knowing whom to displease first: the shrinking number of contributors or the growing number of involuntary beneficiaries. Both parties can vote. To date, a combination of habit and good intentions has favored retention of as many social benefits as are compatible with national resources and strategies. But in the past few years another factor in the welfare debate has threatened to distort national political judgment out of all proportion to its size. This is the so-called immigrant question.

If there is one element in the present European situation which alone ensures that a post-1989 Europe has no prospect of reproducing the successes of the post-1945 era, it is the presence—or, rather, popular resentment at the presence—of immigrants. This is especially ironic since these immigrants (or their parents and grandparents, for many of those who are still regarded as immigrants in Germany or France or Britain were in fact born there) were assiduously encouraged to leave the West Indies, West Africa, or the Near East and southern Europe and come to countries where their unskilled or semiskilled labor was desperately needed in old industries and new services alike. In the mid-1950s most of Western Europe had suffered a triple demographic shortfall brought on by the losses of the First World War, the shortage of babies born during that war, and the second round of civil and military deaths in the Second World War. In West Berlin, following the building of the Wall, Turks were actively recruited to fill jobs once held by East Germans. As much as anyone, these immigrants helped bring about Western Europe's economic miracle, not least because they were young and cheap; for in many cases they came to Europe after completing their education, but long before they would become a burden upon the health services. They were the best bargain Europe ever made and the final, enduring advantage of imperial conquest.

As a result of this immigration, Western Europe in the early 1960s had an excess of immigrants over emigrants for the first time in this century. The net annual average immigration between 1960 and 1964, at the height of the influx, for the six countries of the EEC and the United Kingdom was 569,000; the figures would be higher but for Italy, a country of net emigration until the early seventies; the French figures, it should be noted, are distorted for a few years after 1959 by the involuntary "repatriation" of former colonial families, the *pieds noirs* from North Africa, following war and Algerian independence. By 1973, the high point of the "foreign presence" in Western Europe, the EEC nations together with Austria, Switzerland, Norway, and Sweden had some 7.5 million foreign workers, of whom nearly 5 million were in France and Germany, constituting about 10 percent of the labor force in both countries.

Despite a sharp falloff in numbers since then, because governments have restricted immigration for both economic and political reasons, the "immigrant" presence has remained significant. According to data from 1990, about 6.1 percent of the German population, 6.4 percent of the French, 4.3 percent of the Dutch, and 3.3 percent of the British are foreigners. These figures do not include naturalized immigrants or locally born children of foreigners (though in some countries—notably Germany —these continue to be counted as foreigners and lack full citizens' rights). Many of these "guest workers" were indeed working; despite endemic and structural unemployment in the host country they could usually find low-paying work, having become something of a necessary presence at the very bottom of the European economic ladder (foreigners who had come as refugees, on the other hand, did not on the whole find regular employment).

The last time a steady flow of migrant labor had found its way into Western Europe, in the decade following World War I, it became a target for political exploitation the moment circumstances permitted. The experience is now being repeated. More than any other single issue, it is "immigrants" who have attracted the attention and the anger of politicians and voters over the past decade. For the first postwar generation, in the fifties, immigrants were an exotic source of cheap labor at a time when everyone was doing well. For the baby boomers, who took prosperity for granted, they and other minorities were all but invisible. But for the insecure and vulnerable generation that has come of age in the last decade, any competition (real or imagined) for housing, education, welfare, and employment is a threat.

To this shift in perspectives another should be added. Prejudice, whether in its traditional European form of anti-Semitism or in more imperial variants, was at a

steep discount after 1945. For a long time after the war
Western Europe was a privileged arena within which
racist language was frowned on, extremist parties unknown, the right of asylum widely recognized, and *that*
past, the recent history of discrimination, exploitation,
and extermination, vigorously rejected. That this was a
transformation can be confirmed by any comparison
with, for example, the press and literature of the 1930s,
in France and Belgium no less than in Italy and Germany. It was all the easier to effect because it conformed
well to the self-account of the "new Europe," which thus
appeared to practice in its open-door policies what it
preached in its legal conventions. But it came to an end
with embarrassing haste as politicians across the legitimate spectrum scrambled to recapture the political
initiative from anti-immigrant demagogues, thereby implicitly authorizing the beginnings of a return to bad
old ways.

Just how far this process has now gone may be seen
in recent opinion polls in France. In May 1989 one-fifth
of the electorate of former President Valéry Giscard
d'Estaing's party, the UDF, and 28 percent of Jacques
Chirac's Gaullist supporters pronounced themselves
"globally in agreement" with the ideas about immigrants expressed in the program of Jean-Marie Le Pen's
Front National. In 1991 the figures were 38 percent and
50 percent respectively. And if the Communist and Socialist voters were less sympathetic, that was only because a significant number of them had already switched

their allegiance to Le Pen (in the presidential elections of 1995, Le Pen won 30 percent of the votes of the employed working class, the Socialist candidate Lionel Jospin obtaining just 21 percent).

The point to note here is that by the end of the 1980s a large minority of mainstream voters in France saw nothing unrespectable about expressing agreement with policies that twenty years before would have been regarded as unacceptably close to Fascism (among the proposals in Le Pen's November 1991 list of "Fifty measures to be taken on immigration" was one to withdraw previously granted naturalizations, an act of retroactive injustice last practiced in France under the government of Philippe Pétain). In the words of Bruno Mégret, one of Le Pen's closest colleagues, the "old taboos" are at an end. And what is true for France applies no less in Italy, where the recycled neo-Fascists have recently served in government; in the Netherlands, where extreme nationalist groups are now part of the political mainstream; in Austria, where Jörg Haider's far-right Freedom Party got 22 percent of the vote in the December 1995 national elections; and even in Germany, where increasing restrictions on guest workers and other would-be immigrants have been imposed "in their own interest."

The politics of immigration will not soon subside, because outsiders are a permanent presence in Western Europe, and a visible one. Cross-continental and inter-continental migrations are once again a feature of European society, and local fears and prejudices will ensure that they continue to be seen as a disruptive and politically exploitable element; equally strong feeling in earlier decades against Polish or Italian or Portuguese immigrants was eventually muted as their children, distinguished by neither religion nor language nor color, blended into the social landscape. These advantages of cultural and physical invisibility are not available to their successors from Turkey, Africa, India, or the Antilles. There is very little tradition in Europe of effective assimilation—or, alternatively, "multiculturalism"—when it comes to truly foreign communities; the assimilationist traditions of France, for example, rest on a high and continuing public intolerance for difference of any kind.[5] Immigrants and their children will join the ranks of the "losers" in the competition for Western Europe's reduced resources.

They will not, however, be alone. The gap between rich and poor in Western Europe is widening once again. In Britain the correlation between life expectancy, cause of death, and social class is now stronger than at any time since the 1930s. After fifteen years of regressive

5. Of which the ridiculous Loi Toubon, forbidding the use of any foreign words in official business, or in publicly subsidized transactions, is an absurd but representative instance. Recognized "associations for the defense of the French language" may now sue for damages if English is used, e.g., when a French teacher on French soil addresses non-French-speaking students from the United States.

social and economic policies, many of the gains of the welfare state have been wiped out: the distribution of wealth is as uneven as it was in 1949, with the bottom 20 percent having just 8 percent of the national income, while the top fifth has 42 percent. In 1989 there were upward of 400,000 homeless people, a figure that would have been unthinkable in Britain thirty years before.[6] Within the European Union as a whole, wealth and resources are unevenly distributed by region as well as by class—Greece, Portugal, and all of Spain except Catalonia have an annual per capita national product less than three-quarters that of the *average* for the Union as a whole. Portuguese national productivity per capita was just half the European average in 1991.

The complicated, expensive systems of regional aid that the European Union put in place within and between countries amount, under these circumstances, to a form of institutionalized outdoor relief—constantly correcting for market deformations that have concentrated wealth and opportunity in the wealthy northwestern core without doing anything to alter the causes of the disparity. Southern Europe, the peripheries (Ireland, Portugal, Greece), the economic underclass, and the "immigrants" thus constitute a community of the disadvantaged for whom the EU is the only source of relief on the one hand—for without succor from Brussels

6. See Eric J. Hobsbawm, *The Age of Extremes* (New York, 1994), p. 406.

much of Western Europe, from depressed former mining communities to unprofitable peasant villages, would be in even worse trouble than it is—and the object of envy and resentment on the other. For where there are losers there are also winners.

To see "Europe" at work one has only to spend a few hours in the multinational triangle constituted by the cities of Saarbrücken (Germany), Metz (France), and Luxembourg. Here prosperous citizens of three countries move freely across all-but-vanished frontiers, residing in one state, working in another, shopping in a third. People, employment, commodities, and entertainment move freely back and forth among languages and states, seemingly unconscious of the historic tensions and enmities that marked this very region in the quite recent past. Local children continue to grow up in France, Germany, or Luxembourg and learn their histories according to national instructional rites; but what they learn no longer corresponds very well with what they see; all in all, that is to the good. The natural logic of the union of the Saarland with Lorraine has been achieved, not under the auspices of the German high command or of a French army of occupation, but following the benign designs of the European Commission.

*C'est magnifique, mais ce n'est pas l'Europe.* Or, to be fair, it is indeed "Europe," but from a very distinctive angle. For of what does *this* Europe consist, geographically speaking? What are its capitals, and where are its institutions? The Commission and its civil service sit in

Brussels. The Parliament and its committees meet in Strasbourg and Luxembourg. The European Court of Justice is in The Hague. Crucial decisions regarding further unification of the "thing" are taken at Maastricht, while an agreement to pool frontier regulations and the policing of aliens is signed at Schengen. All six towns, within close and easy reach of one another, lie athwart a line running from the North Sea to the Alps, the very line that formed the centerpiece and primary communications route of the Carolingian monarchy.

The heart (and, some would add, the soul) of today's European Union, then, echoes almost to the kilometer the first west European empire. Extended a little to the east and west—from Reims to Aachen, say, or perhaps Paris to Cologne—and carried south across the western Alpine passes into Lombardy, it is the Europe of the twelfth-century urban renaissance. There is nothing wrong with this—there is even something rather satisfying in the thought that Charlemagne and his heirs would have felt at home in the European Union; but the instinctive, atavistic (and politically calculated) location of these modern capitals of "Europe" should serve as a cautionary reminder that what is true about today's Europe may not be very new, and what is proclaimed as new perhaps not wholly true.

There is another curiously premodern feature of Europe today. Most of its "winners," those people and places which have done well from the emergence of a union and which associate their prosperity with an emphatically European identity, are best described in terms not of nation-states but of regions. The great success stories of contemporary Europe are Baden-Württemberg, in southwestern Germany; the Rhône-Alpes region of France; Lombardy; and Catalonia. All but one of these super-regions (none of which contains the national capital of its country) are grouped around Switzerland, as though wishing they could somehow clamber out of the constraints of their association with poorer areas of Italy, Germany, and France and become, by proximity and affinity, prosperous little Alpine republics themselves. Their disproportionate prosperity and economic power are striking. The Rhône-Alpes region, together with greater Paris, accounts for about a third of French gross domestic product. Catalonia, in 1993, was responsible for 19 percent of Spain's GDP, 23 percent of Spanish exports, and one-quarter of all foreign investment; its per capita income was some 20 percent higher than the average for Spain as a whole.

This economic disproportionality, in the Catalan case, further stirs the already well-fueled fires of regional separatism. Resentful at Franco's deliberate encouragement of Castilian immigration to Barcelona and its region (itself a strategy aimed at diluting the well-justified anti-Franco sentiments of Catalan nationalists), Catalans took advantage of the restoration of democracy in Spain to assert their separate identity. A 1983 Law of Linguistic Normalization made Catalan the "dominant language of instruction" in local schools, while still permitting

Spanish to be used in the schoolroom. Ten years later the Generalitat (Catalonia's governing body) gave a further turn to the screw by decreeing the *exclusive* use of Catalan in school for children to the age of eight. This assertion of a national (and non-Spanish) identity was part of continuing efforts to restrict the Madrid authorities' redistribution of tax and other revenues from Catalonia to some of the poorer of Spain's seventeen "autonomous communities."

The Catalan case is perhaps extreme, in that advocates of autonomy there can point not just to economic self-sufficiency but also to an ancient and unbroken linguistic heritage. Most of the fifteen regionally administered areas of Italy can claim no such linguistic distinctiveness; yet together with the five "autonomous districts" (Valle d'Aosta, Trentino–Alto Adige, Friuli–Venezia Giulia, Sardinia, and Sicily, the first three of which contain significant linguistic minorities) they are no less adamant in their demands for separate representation and autonomous powers. The German *Länder* are all tireless in their efforts to maintain and increase their prerogatives (in education, environment, tourism, and culture especially) by restricting their dealings with the national government in Bonn and referring directly to the European authorities at Brussels whenever possible. Some of these German regions, such as Saxony and Bavaria, can look to a long national past of their own; others are recent administrative inventions. In France, too, many of today's official regions lack historical pedigree; they are postwar inventions, or new combinations of existing but defunct administrative units. In the French case the administrative decentralizations that brought them into being are less than two decades old; real power and decision-making initiative remain with Paris.

Nonetheless, real or invented, the wealthy regions of Western Europe have discovered a strong interest in associating with one another, directly or through the institutions of Europe. And in the nature of things, it is an interest that puts them ever more at odds with the older nation-state of which they are still constituent parts. This is not a new source of disagreement. In Italy the resentment of northerners at sharing the country with a "parasitic" south is a theme as old as the state itself. Flemish national separatism in Belgium, which flourished under the Nazis and for that very reason was somewhat quiescent after the war, has benefited in recent years from the economic decline of industrial Wallonia; we Flemings, the argument now runs, claim not just linguistic equality and separate administration but our own (non-Belgian) identity—and state.

The pattern here is not confined to Western Europe. By the late 1980s the northern peoples or regions of unified nation-states were becoming, in their own eyes, the advanced economic sectors in states that were staffed and even governed largely by people from an impoverished but politically privileged south. Through the accidents (and misfortunes) of history, they were the victims in a relationship that bound them for no enduring reason to semi-alien communities that dominated and depended upon them at the same time. This is how Catalans, the Italian Northern League, Flemish separatists, and even some Scots see their condition. It also describes Czech attitudes to Slovaks before the "velvet divorce," and is a version of the causes and justification for the breakup of Yugoslavia that is popular among some politicians and intellectuals in Croatia and, especially, Slovenia.

The common feature of the separatist claim in these cases in that "we" are "European"—modern, prosperous, tax-paying, better-educated, linguistically and/or culturally distinct northerners—while "they"—the rural, backward, lazy, Mediterranean, subsidized "south"—are somehow less so. The logical imperative of a "European" identity that distinguishes itself from undesirable neighbors with whom it shares a state is to look to an alternative pole of authority, choosing "Brussels" over Rome, Madrid, Belgrade, or even Brussels itself.[7] The appeal of

7. In the Belgian case there is something absurdly counterintuitive about describing the French-speaking inhabitants of Wallonia as "less European" than their Dutch-speaking neighbors to the north. But the Walloons are without question more *Belgian*—if only because they, their economy, and their language dominated the state for so many decades. It is thus consistent with the broader pattern that Flemish separatists should cloak their own nationalist and sometimes racist rhetoric in a shroud of Euro-talk.

"European Union" under these circumstances is that of cosmopolitan modernity against old-fashioned, restrictive (and, it is suggested, artificial and imposed) national constraints. This in turn may account for the special attraction of "Europe" to many of the younger intelligentsia in these lands.

The Soviet Union once attracted many western intellectuals as a promising combination of philosophical ambition and administrative power, and "Europe" has some of the same seductive appeal. For its admirers, as for many politicians and businessmen in the advanced regions of western and central Europe, the "Union" is the latest heir to the enlightened despotism of the last great reforming era before the coming of national states. For what is "Brussels," after all, if not a renewed attempt to achieve that ideal of efficient, universal administration, shorn of particularisms and driven by rational calculation and the rule of law, which the great eighteenth-century monarchs—Catherine, Frederick, Maria Theresa, and Joseph II—strove to institute in their ramshackle lands? The very rationality of the European Community ideal has made it appealing, especially to that educated professional intelligentsia which, in east and west alike, sees in "Brussels" an escape from hidebound practices and provincial backwardness, much as eighteenth-century lawyers, traders, and writers appealed to enlightened monarchs over the heads of reactionary parliaments and diets.

But there is a price to be paid for this reorientation

of Europe, this new magnetic pole for its most successful constituents. If "Europe" stands for the winners, the wealthy regions and subregions of existing states, who speaks for the losers—the "south," the poor, linguistically, educationally, or culturally disadvantaged, underprivileged, or despised Europeans who don't live in golden triangles along vanished frontiers and for whom "Brussels" is at best an administrative abstraction, at worst a politically targeted object of fear and loathing? The risk is that what remains to *these* Europeans is the "nation," or, more precisely, nationalism. This is not the same as the national separatism of Catalans or the regional self-advancement of Lombards; it is about preserving the nineteenth-century state as a defense against change, not about breaking it up in favor of smaller units for which change, in association with a larger, transnational unit, is attractive.

Defensive nationalist rhetoric works best in depressed regions, or in those with no marked regional consciousness, where angry and frightened voters can always be mobilized against real and imagined foreign threats to jobs and "way of life." In itself that is nothing new, and in eastern Europe it has since 1989 become the familiar form of populist politics.[8] Meanwhile, in western Europe

8. The Polish journalist Konstanty Gebert has noted that the syntax of Communism and nationalism is essentially the same, whereas liberal democracy is, as it were, linguistically distinctive. Despite the gulf separating the universal values and goals of socialism and the particularistic, exclusionary politics of

the nation-state had seemed to be on a path to gentle extinction. With political and social stability assured by a consensus that bound together Socialists and Conservatives, Social Democrats and Christian Democrats, and with its primary historical task—national defense—externally guaranteed, the characteristic outlines of the modern European state had become blurred. Maintenance of internal order and external security had ostensibly been replaced by management of resources; since more and more of these were generated and distributed by multinational agents (private and public), the conventions of national allegiance seemed to be at a discount. With each new generation, "nationalism" seemed increasingly anachronistic, its invocation at sporting competitions endearingly (or disturbingly, depending on the sport) out of place. In polite circles criticism of "Europe" seemed somehow mildly indecent, indicative of a failure to remember what Enzensberger has called the recent "European suicide attempt" and the lessons it taught.

All that is now changing. Just as an obsession with "growth" has left a moral vacuum at the heart of some modern nations, so the abstract, materialist quality of the idea of Europe is proving insufficient to legitimate its own institutions and retain popular confidence. The mere objective of unification is not enough to capture

---

nationalism, he is clearly right, as Messrs. Milošević, Tudjman, Mečiar, and the people who elected them can confirm.

the imagination and allegiance of those left behind by change, the more so in that it is no longer accompanied by a convincing promise of indefinitely extended well-being. Since 1989 there has been a return of memory and with it, and benefiting from it, a revival of the national units that framed and shaped that memory and give meaning to the collective past. This process threatens to undermine and substitute for the inadequacies of the Europe-without-a-past. Thus for many years, in France or Germany, nationalist rhetoric was discredited by its close association with the memory and language of Nazism or of the Pétain regime ("Travail, Famille, Patrie"). This self-censure has all but disappeared except among an older generation of left-wing intellectuals, nowadays largely ignored. After two decades during which identification with Europe seemed to be replacing association with a nation, "Euro-barometer" opinion polls are suggesting a reverse trend. In Germany, Denmark, Spain, Portugal, and the U.K. a majority or near majority of those asked in 1994 saw themselves in the coming years as identifying *uniquely* with their own nation.

Why is this? In the first place, "Europe" is too large and too nebulous a concept around which to forge any convincing human community. And it is not psychologically realistic to posit, along lines favored by the German writer Jürgen Habermas, a local and supra-national duality of communities around which allegiances may form, prudently shorn of the dangerous emphasis on "identity" associated with the historical national unit. It does not work. It is also an echo of the reductivist fallacy, the curiously nineteenth-century belief shared by classical economists and Marxists alike, that social and political institutions and affinities naturally and necessarily follow economic ones. There is no doubt that production, commerce, and finance are now organized globally, and that continental, interregional organisms are the likely future of European economic life. But we have no good reason to believe that other aspects of human existence can or should follow suit. Ever more harmonized trading networks and empire-wide commercial links did nothing to bind together the centrifugal components of late-nineteenth-century Austria-Hungary.

Within the last two generations western Europeans have lost or abandoned many of the traditional integrative institutions of modern public life. The role of family, church, school, or army is negligible today in most western countries, when compared to the situation half a century ago. Political parties and trade unions no longer perform the organizational and pedagogic function they served in Europe for more than a century. At the same time that economic pressures are tempting governments to reduce the acquired benefits of public welfare, the familiar building blocks of what the French call *solidarité* are dropping away. It may well be that the nation—with the community of memory that it represents and the state that embodies it, with its familiar and appropriately scaled frame—is the only remaining, as well as the best-adapted, source of collective and communal identification. Given the dramatic collapse of the great abstract universal goals of the Socialist utopia, and the untenable promise of an ever larger *and* ever more prosperous continental union, the virtues of a social unit based on geographical propinquity and rooted in the past rather than the future have perhaps been understated. In any case, more attention to the virtues of the nation and its state on the part of respectable politicians (and, by contrast, less attention to the wonders of "Europe") might help retrieve it from the arms of its more extremist suitors.

One way or another, the state is likely to be needed in the future. The conventional nation-state is going to be much sought after in the next few years to assist in the preservation of the social fabric, whether by coercion or redistributive intervention, however unpopular this may be in the privileged "super-regions." It is not only in former Communist states that the self-regulating virtues of the unrestricted market appear to have been oversung. The much-maligned "interventionist state" may have been prematurely consigned to the dustbin of history; it might be better not to partition, decentralize, or reduce its capacities too much and too soon. The years after World War II saw the dramatic restoration of the social and economic functions of nation-states in Western Europe, and this process was aided by the "Europeanizing" of their problems; the years after 1989 will require a rehabilitation of the nation-state's political and cultural credibility if Europe itself is to remain afloat.[9]

It is not, after all, as though the "nation-state" were an ancient political form that has had its day. It is, in fact, the most modern of political institutions. Even the political institutions of long-established countries such as France or Britain or the Netherlands acquired their modern function and political shape only in the course of the nineteenth century. And the nation-state is peculiarly well adapted to the modern need for civic responsibility and active and effective political participation. Subnational regions or "micro-states" inevitably look beyond their frontiers for allies and assistance to enable them to achieve objectives for which they lack domestic resources. Or they are vulnerable to absorption by a larger, aggressive, expanding neighboring country. Oversized transnational units suffer a perennial "democratic deficit"—which is precisely the charge to which the European Union is now exposed and to which it will remain especially susceptible. They may or may not function well in the administration of things, but when

9. For the argument that the European Community came into being, functionally speaking, in order to save the domestic economies of its members, see Alan Milward, *The European Rescue of the Nation-State* (Berkeley and Los Angeles, 1992).

it comes to governing people they are too large, too distant, and therefore inevitably break up into their constituent parts. It is as well to ensure that those parts have not been weakened beyond repair.

The gravest weakness of the nation-state itself is its implicitly exclusive quality: France for the French, etc. Historically, this characteristic defect has been the source of its decline. Multinational states (Yugoslavia, Belgium) break apart; homogeneous single-nation states (Poland, Portugal) are the uncommon (sometimes tragic) product of history and cannot be invented; "stateless" minorities everywhere are weak or persecuted and seek their own territory, of necessity at someone else's expense. If "Europe" were indeed a solution to this dilemma—if the free movement of peoples, abolition of frontiers, and intermixing of nations could really be achieved—it would certainly be worth almost any price in institutional overkill and economic inequality. If "Europe" now means a true, definitively cosmopolitan solution to the parochial provincialism and dangerously exclusivist cultures of nation-states, then it would be a desirable goal, for all its imperfections.

Unfortunately, this is not the case. Far from opening up, "Europe" since 1989 has been steadily if somewhat furtively engaged in closing in upon itself. For the reasons I have suggested, the European Union cannot realistically promise its members a future as secure and as prosperous as its past. The unique combination of circumstances that prevailed in the Community's early years has passed and will not come again. It is even less likely that this same Union will open itself to new and poorer members on anything like the terms hitherto accorded. The recently touted German idea of a small inner core of European states moving at full speed toward integration and setting demanding macro-economic criteria for membership in their club is merely the latest evidence that the future of Europe will be on German terms or not at all. It is unlikely that Italy, Spain, or even Britain will ever qualify for such an exclusive club, and even more absurd to envisage Poland or Slovakia doing so. Actually, *no one* except Luxembourg really qualifies according to the criteria set out in various position papers from the Christian Democrats, but to make the idea even semi-plausibly "European," Germany, France, Belgium, and the Netherlands have to be in, rules or no rules. Such subterfuges—"hard core," "fast track," "Partnership for Peace," "economic areas," conventions, agreements, and promises—are all devices to postpone or avoid the impossible choice of either saying no to newcomers or else expanding the Union on equal terms. Almost no one in eastern Europe is fooled by this; but having no better options they choose to believe in their own hopes.

Seen from inside, and from the west, however, the Union, despite its recent expansion, seems in fact to be shrinking; for most of its members today the EU represents the Atlantic and Mediterranean fringe of a continent that suddenly seems rather large and very problematic. Even Germany, more conscious of the other Europe than most of her partners and always tempted to straddle the continent, makes no bones about the distinction between "us" and "them": in 1994 Bonn allocated DM 11 million to support the few hundred thousand remaining *Volksdeutschen* in Romania, while simultaneously paying the Romanian government substantial sums to take back those of "its" Gypsies who had found their way to Germany. From the outside the European Union remains a source of hope and opportunity as well as security and stability for all the peoples to its east and south. From the inside, however, it seems more like an embattled fortress.

Hence the symbolic importance of the agreement signed at Schengen among sovereign nations (Germany, France, the Benelux countries, Spain, and Portugal, with Italy a candidate member) to abolish their common frontiers, harmonize visa and immigration regulations, and accept controls exercised at one frontier as valid for all. A person allowed into Portugal would thus be free to roam as far as the Polish frontier, unquestioned and unmolested; the very incarnation of a postnational Europe. In practice, of course, the agreement means something quite different. It means that whichever state has the most draconian and exclusive immigration and/or labor laws will be able to impose its requirements on all

others—a sort of highest common factor of discrimina-
tory political arithmetic. The regulations will be enforced through a continent-wide pooling of data, a kind
of Interpol for foreigners, refugees, and immigrants, so
that the policing powers of this multi-state will far ex-
ceed those of its constituent parts. In its finished form,
assuming that Italy joins—the Scandinavian nations
have already agreed to do so—the Schengen arrangement will unite the European Union within an
exclusion zone running, once again, from Gdansk to
Trieste.

The object of Schengen is to make of Poland, the
Czech Republic, Slovakia, Hungary, Croatia, and Slovenia, as well as the Mediterranean Sea, a sort of demographic *limes*, tampon states that would absorb and block
the westward or northward movement of desperate
peoples—their own or those to the south and east of
them. This casts some doubt upon the plausibility of
promises made about the eventual eastward extension
of the benefits of Union—if Schengen *could* without difficulty be extended east and south, after all, it would
not be needed in the first place. It also points up the
European Union's most immediate concern today, which
is to protect itself against the economic and political
risks of further in-migration. Since this is exactly what
nationalist politicians in Western European countries
would have their own governments do if they could, a
post-Schengen European Union hardly offers a very in-

teresting alternative to the conventional national state. Perhaps these restrictionist practices, like so much else in Europe today, are less obviously unappetizing when undertaken on behalf of "ever-closer union" rather than in the name of the nation.

This is not the first time that a hitherto expansionist Europe has felt obliged to contract in the face of external impediments. Contraction has often been the condition for, even the definition of, greater collective consciousness. From the barbarian invasions to the Iron Curtain via Arabs and Ottomans, outside pressure has historically forced unity upon Europe, at the cost of reduced ambition. Global decolonization, too, sharpened *European* consciousness, when it obliged first the French and Dutch, then the British, to acknowledge their reduced means and make a continental virtue of diminished imperial necessity. True, European contractionist practice is now somewhat at variance with its preaching, but no more so than under the Most Catholic kings and emperors of the early modern era, who made tactical alliances with Protestant republics and Muslim sultans alike, according to need.

This long history of expansion and contraction helps to explain why Western Europe's present dilemma seems hardly novel, and perhaps long predictible. Herder, in the mid-eighteenth century, was already warning of the rumbling of "wild peoples in Eastern Europe," announcing two centuries of German fear of demographic immersion.[10] The anticipated "invasion" of southern Europe by desperate refugees and work-seekers from North Africa, the Middle East, and the Balkans has been a steady theme of conservative and nationalist writing in Spain, France, and Italy for three decades. What is perhaps new is that northern and southern Europeans have pooled not just their resources but also their fears. France and its Mediterranean friends have agreed to be understanding about Germany's concerns over the future of central Europe, while Germany has consented to an increase in Europe's aid to the "south," so as to encourage and assist the countries of the non-European Mediterranean fringe in keeping their problems at home.

Warned or not, the cosseted, amnesiac Europe of the 1949–89 years remained largely oblivious to signs of the coming crises. It was able to continue making all manner of future promises because it ran very little risk of being taken at its word. It is the rapid sequence of events since 1989 that has made the subsequent process of retrenchment seem a little unsavory, the compulsion

10. See Larry Wolff, *Inventing Eastern Europe: The Map of Civilization on the Mind of the Enlightenment* (Stanford, 1994), p. 365ff. Wolff also cites the work of William Sloane (*The Balkans: A Laboratory of History*, 1914), who warned that there would eventually "be forced upon Western Europe some kind of closer union for protection against a hostile invasion of inferior civilisation composed of Slavic stock, Greek Catholicism and Oriental government."

to continue holding out great vistas of future expansion clashing with an urgent sense of impending difficulties and the need to retreat into "fortress Europe."[11] Whatever else this means, it indicates clearly that in its *strong* form the idea of "Europe" has had its day. Its place in our present political dilemmas is broadly comparable to that of the rudimentary organs of which Charles Darwin wrote in the *Origin of Species* that they "may be compared with the letters in a word, still retained in the spelling but become useless in the pronunciation, but which serve as a clue in seeking for the derivation."

11. "The more our peninsula moves back into the centre of world politics and of the market, the more a new kind of Euro-centrism will gain ground. A slogan that was copyrighted by Joseph Goebbels has reappeared in public debate: 'Fortress Europe.' It was once meant in a military sense; it has returned as an economic and demographic concept. A Europe in renewal will do well to remind itself of a Europe in ruins, from which it is separated by only a few decades" (H.-M. Enzensberger).

# AFTERWORD

Discussion today of the prospects for Europe tends to oscillate rather loosely between Pangloss and Cassandra, between bland assurance and dire prophecy. I have argued that the likelihood that the European Union will fulfill its own promises of ever-closer union, while remaining open to new members on the same terms, is slim indeed. But it does not follow that everything so far achieved will therefore come crashing down, or that it should count for nothing. The European Union is a remarkable accomplishment, albeit not quite *so* remarkable as its advocates suggest. That, after all, is why nearly everyone wants to join it.

But however desirable in principle, an ever-closer bonding of the nations of Europe is impossible in practice, and it is therefore perhaps imprudent to promise it. In arguing for a more modest assessment of Euro-prospects, and for a continuing recognition of the proper place of the traditional state, I don't wish to suggest that there is something *inherently* superior about national institutions over others. But we should recognize the reality of nations and states, and note the risk that, when neglected, they become an electoral resource of virulent nationalists.

It may also be true that the old-fashioned nation-state is a better form in which to secure collective loyalties, protect the disadvantaged, enforce a fairer distribution of resources, and compensate for disruptive transnational economic patterns. To that extent a medium-sized geographical and demographic unit has certain enduring advantages. The reorganization of much of Europe is already a fact—Belgium, Italy, Spain, and of course Yugoslavia will certainly not revert to their previous constitutional and administrative shape. But there are good reasons to abstain from encouraging any further the subdivision of existing states, whether in the name of self-determination or on behalf of administrative Euro-federalism. The resulting backlash may far outweigh the benefits.

Should the European Union take in the countries of eastern Europe? There is no definitive answer to the question of where "Europe" properly ends, of how the *telos* of a united continent translates onto a map. On the other hand, for reasons I have tried to suggest, the countries of former Communist Europe will never join the rest of the European Union on an equal footing. On the contrary, and offensive as it sounds, for the foreseeable future it would be an act of charity, economically speaking, for the EU to absorb the countries to its east on such terms. But would it not, perhaps, be in western

Europe's self-interest to make the sacrifice notwithstanding (always supposing it can afford to do so)?

Let us set aside the issue of cultural affinity—whether, that is, western Europe is lacking a vital part of itself if it is in any way separated from central or eastern Europe. That is a perennially interesting topic but not to the planners in Brussels, for whom "Europe" is increasingly about more mundane, material forms of union—most recently, the objective of a single currency. The perceived self-interest of western Europe today lies in securing itself against demographic and economic threats to its east and south. As for threats of a more conventional sort, it is an unspoken assumption of all European defense planners that Russia remains the only significant military threat to the rest of Europe. That may or may not be so. What is even less clear is whether Russia will be more or less threatening if the borders of a non-Russian European union are pushed nearer to its present frontier. That the major states of western and central Europe have the same interest they have always had in maintaining buffer states to separate them from Russia is clear. But whether these perform their geo-strategic role better in or out of a formal Union remains an open question for many western diplomats.

West European debate is also concentrated, narcissistically, upon the workings of the European Union itself. The interminable debates about widening and deepening that union have since the signing of the

Maastricht Treaty begun to boil down to a simple problem of decision-taking procedures. Should collective European undertakings be decided by unanimous agreement (as now) or by majority voting? And in the latter case, how should majorities be construed, and how binding are their decisions to be? Helmut Kohl, the late François Mitterrand, and their political advisers favored the introduction of a system of majority voting, to eliminate the risk of deadlock that would arise from any attempt to meet the needs and demands of so many member-states; the British, supported by some of the smaller member states, favor retention of the veto (the same veto wielded by Charles de Gaulle to keep the British out in January 1963!) precisely to prevent decisions being taken against their interests—and indeed, to prevent the taking of too many decisions of any sort at all. It is not by chance that these conflicts have come to the fore. In the Europe of Fifteen it is going to be near-impossible to find overwhelming majorities, much less unanimity, for decisions requiring hard choices.

This will be especially true in matters of defense and foreign policy, arenas in which the European Union has hitherto been inactive (although its senior members have of course been full partners in NATO, France partially excepted). Despite the United States' effective, if belated, intervention in Bosnia, the option of military quiescence is no longer open to Europe; for reasons of domestic political pressure and economic retrenchment, the United States cannot be counted on to involve itself in European affairs whenever its services are required. The European Union has utterly failed to bring its members together for any common policy or action in military or foreign affairs. And what has proven difficult for fifteen members would be out of the question for a larger number still. The result is predictable. Where the European Union and its forebears once resembled the UN —taking unanimous decisions on areas of common interest and agreeing to disagree, or just not decide, on difficult or divisive topics—it will now begin to look like the League of Nations, with members simply opting out of decisions from which they dissent. The moral and political damage that can be done when a single member forces unanimous indecision upon the whole—*vide* the Greek refusal to recognize Macedonia, or Italy's insistence that Slovenia be excluded from consideration for EU membership until long-standing but trivial frontier disputes between the two countries have been addressed—would be nothing compared to a refusal by Britain or France, for example, to accept the foreign-policy commitment of a majority composed of Germany and its smaller supporters.

What, then, of western Europe's general interest in stability, in guaranteeing countries like Hungary or Slovakia against their own internal demons? This is in fact the strongest argument eastern Europeans can offer in support of their candidacy for admission to the EU— protect us against ourselves, against the domestic consequences of a failed "post-Communist transition"—and it is particularly persuasive for their neighbors immediately to the west, notably Germany. But it is a purely prudential argument, which is why the EU has tried to meet it by the offer of partial membership, interim affiliation, and so on, and it raises a hypothetical future problem at a time when the West is preoccupied with real and immediate difficulties. Even if this issue does succeed in prizing open the European door, it will only do so at the cost of a significant dilution of the meaning and practices of union. And it will probably not extend the protective arm of "Europe" beyond the old Habsburg center (Poland, the Czech Republic, Hungary, Slovakia, and perhaps Slovenia), making of the latter a sort of depressed Euro-suburb beyond which "Byzantine" Europe (from Latvia to Bulgaria) will be left to fend for itself, too close to Russia and Russian interests for it to be prudent for the West to make an aggressive show of absorption and engagement.

From now on, Europe will be German-dominated in one of three possible ways: the original (pre-1989) western Europe, but under German leadership—which would be the reluctant preference of most French and Mediterranean-European politicians; pro-German central Europe, with Germany playing the benign role in an expanded Union envisaged for it by its present leadership; anti-German central Europe, with Germany regarded by its neighbors to the south and east as more of a burden and a threat than a benefit. The last two may well end up being one and the same—as a current

Czech joke has it, the country faces just two dangers in the future: that Germany *will* invest heavily, buying up the local economy, and that Germany *won't*, leaving it to stagnate. The unbalanced weight of Germany in European affairs is nothing new, of course. But in contrast to earlier days, it is as much a problem for Germany itself as for its anxious neighbors.

In the years before and immediately after 1989 the leaders of the Federal Republic sought anxiously to reassure France and others that a return to full sovereignty for Germany need not threaten them; since 1990, and with the same objective in mind, a united Germany has been urgently seeking partners for its strategy of expansion into central Europe: acting in concert with fellow members of a European "fast track," Bonn would not seem quite so obviously to be striding out ahead. Thus investments in eastern Europe made by German firms using, for example, Austrian subsidiaries or "fronts" raise less local hackles than those coming directly from the Federal Republic. Just as West German foreign policy before 1989 might be characterized as a triple balancing act, neither favoring nor displeasing Washington, Moscow, or Paris, so post-unification German policy is seeking to follow the logic of Germany's power, and her historical place in central and eastern Europe, without frightening her west European allies or arousing Germans' own fears of revived national ambitions.

The difficulty, as some German writers have noted, is that Germany cannot help destabilizing Europe, its own best intentions notwithstanding. It is for this reason that Günter Grass was so adamantly opposed to unification, and why he remains nervously skeptical about its consequences. The Europe that Adenauer and his contemporaries helped to make, and that in turn allowed the Federal Republic to forge its post-Hitler identity, is now in question, the postwar settlement having come to a close. The more dramatic historical analogies may be misleading—the de facto alliance of Germany with Austria inside the EU would not have the meaning of the *Anschluss* of 1938, and a revival of German expansionism, much less militarism, is not likely in Germany, at least for the foreseeable future. But it remains true, as it has been since 1871, that a powerful Germany in the middle of Europe, with interests of its own, is an unsettling presence for its neighbors.

A recent contribution to *Le Monde* by the British minister with responsibility for Europe managed to devote a whole page to "Building Europe in the 21st century" without *once* mentioning Germany! The minister's unmistakable point was that Europe's future lay in the hands of Britain and France, increasingly reconciled to mutual support by their shared concerns over the direction taken by events; unstated but implied was the idea that both countries had much to lose by a shift to the east in Europe's center of gravity, and by a system of decision-making in which their interests might be diluted by a majority of lesser states. On the other hand, Britain and France are (sometimes) willing and able to take the initiative in diplomatic affairs. And in the coming crisis of the Atlantic alliance, this above all would be the measure of Europe in the coming century.

This argument may be self-serving and in the long tradition of myopic British thinking when it comes to Europe, but it is not for that reason erroneous. A Europe dominated by Germany, in striking contrast to the past, would be characterized above all by its *un*willingness to intervene actively in international affairs. That is because Germany has every interest in merging its own concerns and objectives into the broadest possible international consensus. Whether this will always be so is another matter—the trauma of Nazism cannot continue to weigh upon the German public conscience indefinitely, and there must come a point when German politicians and their electors will be less inhibited about behaving like any other power: sending soldiers abroad, using force or the threat of force to achieve national goals, and so forth. But in the meantime the chief difficulty posed to its members by a German-dominated Europe is a curious sort of inertia, forcing the European community to restrict its collective international interventions to uncontentious issues of an environmental or humanitarian nature.

This, above all else, is the lesson of the Yugoslav tragedy, illustrating as it does the weakness of European initiatives, the compulsion to avoid engagement, and the absence of any recognized collective strategic interest beyond maintaining the status quo. The Europeans, the

French especially, may resent the apparent ease with which U.S. involvement put a temporary end to the conflict in Bosnia, and there has been acerbic comment in the French press, noting that if the United States had wished, it could have achieved its present ends a lot earlier and thereby saved thousands of lives. But the fact remains that the Bosnian imbroglio has revealed the sheer emptiness of the "European" construct, its selfish obsession with fiscal rectitude and commercial advantage.

The war in Yugoslavia since 1991 is also a timely reminder that Germans are not the only people for whom German hegemony in Europe is unwelcome. One of the strongest points in Serbian propaganda, first against Slovenian and Croatian independence and then against external "interference" in Bosnia, has been its claim that Germany and Austria are active and interested parties in forging a restored, "German-Catholic" *Mitteleuropa* and that the whole enterprise of dismantling Yugoslavia is a sort of Teutono-Habsburg plot. Even journalists affiliated with the opposition parties in Belgrade are disposed to give credence to this explanation of the tragedy that has struck their country. Fear of giving hostages to this argument prevented Europe's most powerful state from getting involved actively until four years into the war, and even then the decision to send a small German military contingent—confined to strictly noncombat duties—was only taken against much opposition from intellectual and political (notably Green and Social Democratic) circles in Germany.

This is not to say that the behavior of France or Great Britain has been exemplary. But the French and the British have been constrained to do *something*, however inadequate and even perfidious—hence the dispatch of a small Rapid Reaction Force to Sarajevo in 1995, after it became embarrassingly clear just how ineffectual the UN presence there had become.[1] But because this force was a Franco-British one, and not operating under any sort of "European" aegis, it confirmed another lesson taught by events in the Balkans: just as there is no effective international community, so there is, for international purposes, no European one either. There are merely powers, great and not so great; and for the moment at least, a German-led Europe is not among them. How France and Britain will use the limited international initiative this gives them will depend on what lesson, if any, their governments choose to learn from their Bosnian adventure. But forty years after the Anglo-French humiliation of Suez they are about to rediscover the charms, and burdens, of relative diplomatic autonomy. The United States is no longer looking over their

1. It did not go unremarked in Bosnia, however, that the main objective of this force was to protect other foreign troops (French and British especially) operating under UN authority and exposed to Serbian fire, kidnapping, and blackmail.

shoulder, and "Europe" is no longer a credible bolt-hole.

The years 1945–89 are thus coming to seem more and more like a parenthesis. This does not mean that we are about to return to bad old ways. The past, having once happened, leaves a record and a memory, and that memory is one of the reasons why the things it recalls will not simply be repeated. But it is also true that people can forget to remember—or, perhaps, forget to forget—and that as we move further away from 1945 the reasons why it seemed so important to build something different will be less pressing. That is why we must remind ourselves not just that real gains have been made, but that the European community which helped to make them was a means, not an end.

If we look to European Union as a solution for everything, chanting "Europe" like a mantra, waving the banner of "Europe" in the face of recalcitrant "nationalist" heretics and screaming "Abjure, abjure!," we shall wake up one day to find that far from solving the problems of our continent, the myth of "Europe" has become an impediment to our recognizing them. We shall discover that it has become little more than the politically correct way to paper over local difficulties, as though the mere invocation of the promise of Europe could substitute for solving problems and crises that really affect the place. Few would wish to deny the ontological existence of Europe, so to speak. And there *is* a certain self-fulfilling advantage in speaking of it as though it already existed in some stronger, collective sense—the wish can indeed assist in fathering the thought and has gone some distance in doing so. But some things it cannot do, some problems it cannot address. "Europe" is more than a geographical notion but less than an answer.

# INDEX

Abetz, Otto, 9
Adam of Bremen, 48
Adenauer, Konrad, 15, 89, 98, 136
*Age of Extremes, The* (Hobsbawm), 79*n*
agriculture, 17–23, 32–33, 41
Algeria, 103
*Anschluss*, 136
anti-Fascism, myth of, 84
anti-Semitism, 73, 104
Arendt, Hannah, 15*n*
assimilation, 107
Attlee, Clement, 36
Austria, 3, 4, 26, 48, 77; and EC budget, 91; far right in, 101, 106; Germany and, 135, 136, 138; historical studies in, 84, 85*n*; immigrants in, 103; imperial, 56, 70; in International Steel Cartel, 7; nationalists in, 72; nineteenth-century, 87
Austria-Hungary, 119

baby boom, 99–101, 104
Baden-Württemberg, 111
Balkans, 49, 58, 77, 79*n*, 93, 139; see also specific countries
*Balkans, The* (Sloane), 127*n*
Bavarian Christian Social Union, 36
Belgium, 26, 46, 122–24, 130; and EC budget, 91; in ECSC, 3, 15, 16, 39; Flemish separatism in, 113, 114; German occupation of, 25, 61; in International Steel Cartel, 7; nineteenth-century, 6; postwar, 12, 65; prejudice in, 105; unemployment in, 94–96
Belorussia, 54
Berlin Wall, 43, 89, 93, 102
Bertelsmann Foundation, 92
Bidault, Georges, 11, 98
Bosnia, 76, 132, 138–39
Brandt, Willy, 43
Briand, Aristide, 7–8
Britain, 3, 26, 27, 36, 42, 56, 123, 126; agriculture in, 20; Bosnia and, 139; and Cold War, 28, 29; class differences in, 107–8; coal in, 39; and EC